ONE
FATHER
ONE
FAMILY

ONE FATHER ONE FAMILY

ALGER FITCH

COLLEGE PRESS PUBLISHING CO., Box 1132, Joplin, MO 64802

Library of Congress Catalog Card Number: 90-84917
International Standard Book Number: 0-89900-269-2

TABLE OF CONTENTS

PREFACE

Congratulations for your interest in a biblical study about Christian Unity. Your concern over this topic says, at least, two very complimentary things about you that commend you before God. You want what He desires for His church — its oneness. More than that, to seek what the Bible says reveals that you hold a high view of the Scripture, recognizing the Holy Book as God's revelation to man and not merely the writing of men giving their thoughts about Deity. So together we turn to a source-book that we recognize as revelation and not concealment. We rightly expect that the information gleaned from Bible study will lead to the transformation needed to overcome the division-dilemma that is before us.

And dilemma there is. Our age knows the predicament of split atoms, split personalities, split families and split churches. Mark Twain spoke of the Protestant Church as not only divided, but sub-divided. Romanism concludes that, if Protestantism is to be

7

seen as a branch of the church, it must be recognized as a rotten branch, considering the many pieces into which it has shattered.

How many religious segments are there? The figure we used to hear was approximately 268 denominations in the United States. But the 1984 *Evangelical Dictionary of Theology* records R.L. Omanson's claim that "Today there are an estimated 22,000 (church denominations)."[1] Carol Ward's 1986 *The Christian Sourcebook* puts the figure at "nearly 21,000 different Christian denominations in the world today" and she adds, "an estimated 270 more are formed each year."[2] Obviously most of these factions and fractions are minute in size. With rugged and excessive individualism in the saddle, will the future see each new sect riding off in a different direction? Can the Christian "caste system" of denominationalism be broken?

All people realize that in unity there is strength. Much more power is contained in a fist than a finger. A bundle of sticks tied together are difficult to break, while individually they may be snapped with ease. Citizens of the United States of America pledge allegiance to their flag with the words "one nation under God indivisible" and they recall their constitution's intent "to form a more perfect union." Have you not often quoted the words of G.P. Morris, "United we stand, divided we fall"? Or, perhaps, you rephrased the slogan with Mrs. Oscar Ahlgren at the General Federation of Women's Clubs, "United we stick; divided, we're stuck." No one fears a single locust, but, when they join forces, look out!

"Today, everyone advocates unity," you say. But wait. We also claim no one would oppose motherhood, apple pie or the American flag. Do not the hundreds of thousands of abortions each year, belie the claim that motherhood is sought by all? Hasn't your dietitian warned you about the calories, excessive sugar and high cholesterol in your favorite apple pie? And, surely, you see in the newspapers and on television that flag-burning still goes on. Are there, also, some who see vice and not virture — evil and not good — in unity efforts?

8

No less than Soren Kierkegaard wrote:

> We are always hearing "Let us unite, in order to work for Christianity." And this is meant to be true Christian zeal. Christianity is of another view, it knows very well that this is trickery, for with union Christianity is not advanced, but weakened; and the more union there is, the weaker Christianity becomes.[3]

Kierkegaard is not alone. In the October 10, 1966 issue of *Christianity Today*, dealing with Protestant-Roman Unity, Frank E. Gaebelein avers that "it is highly questionable whether any union could be consummated short of surrender of vital convictions. Such union would be far less desirable than the present state of separation." In the same article, Carl F. H. Henry, the editor of the magazine, wrote, "I do not find in a Bible a basis for discussing 'Protestant-Roman Catholic church unity,' but simply the unity of regenerate believers in the spiritual body of which the crucified and risen Redeemer is authoritative head."

It is becoming clear that denominational "union" and Christian "unity" may not be the same. The church of the Middle Ages was united and powerful to eliminate opposition of every kind. That is not the unity we seek. Those were the dark-ages. On the day of Christ's crucifixion "Herod and Pilate became friends — before this they had been enemies" (Luke 23:2).[4] That is not the joining of forces wanted. The Psalmist, recognizing evil alliances do harm, asks, "Can a corrupt throne be allied with you — one that brings on misery by its decrees? They band together against the righteous and condemn the innocent to death" (Psa. 94:20-21). At Babel God saw a oneness that bode darkness rather than light. You remember His words:

> If as one people speaking the same language they have begun to do this, then nothing they plan to do will be impossible for them. Come, let us go down and confuse their language so they will not understand each other" (Gen. 11:6-7).

In this way marriage is like unity. While, on the whole, matrimony is to be looked upon highly, a lot of people ought not be married. So, while unity is to be favored, not every union would be good.

Unity based on a lie would never please the God of truth. The late Mennonite leader, George Brunk, observed, "While it is true that Christ prayed for the unity of believers, it does not follow, therefore, as some seem to think, that all denominational lines should be broken down and that we should join hands with all that *say* 'Lord, Lord,' whether or not they *do* what the Lord says."

When I go to my travel agent and ask for a flight to Portland, her first inquiry is whether I mean Portland, Oregon or Portland, Maine. Those destinations are hundreds of miles apart. So it is when we go the Bible and want to reach "unity." Do we mean "union" in the ecumenical sense of merging denominations? Or are we really trying to reach "unity" in Christ and his truth? The route to be taken will be determined by the answer to that question.

The word "union" is neither in the Old Testament nor the New Testament. The term "unity" is to be found in Scripture, but only three times. Ephesians 4:3 speaks of "the unity of the Spirit" and the same Pauline epistle in 4:13 predicts a time when Christ's body will "reach unity in the faith and in the knowledge of the Son of God" (The Greek word is ἑνότης, meaning oneness, unanimity). The Old Testament Psalmist sings of "How good and pleasant it is when brothers live together in unity" (Psa. 133:1). The Hebrew word is *yachad*, meaning unitedness, to be or to become one, to join or unite. While we admit that the word unity is seldom found in the Scriptures, the idea of one people of God permeates the Bible's pages. It can be correctly affirmed that reconciliation (ἀποκαταλλάσσω) is the central theme of Heaven's Book, as it tells the good-news "that God was reconciling the world to himself in Christ" (II Cor. 5:19, cp. Eph. 2:16; Col. 1:20). This idea of unity runs like a silver thread from the *alpha* of Genesis to the *omega* of Revelation.

The challenge can not be avoided. Can the church bring

10

reconciliation to our divided world until it is reconciled? Lesslie Newbigen, writing on the atoning work of the cross, cries out that "Our divisions are a public contradiction of that atonement."[5] Is not a divided church a contradiction? Does not the New Testament know only one saving event and one people of God? Division in the Christian ranks has been called perceptively, "the devil's masterpiece." The truth can not be put more tersely. Division has been Satan's most successful tool in hindering the triumph of the gospel over infidelity. We can safely assert that many have been saved in spite of denominationalism, but none because of it. Will the day ever come when, without fingers crossed or minds shutting out reality, we can sing the line of the hymn "Onward, Christian Soldiers" that rings out, "We are not divided; All one body we, One in hope and doctrine, One in charity"?

This book is written with the conviction that God is able. With God it is impossible for the impossible to be impossible. Disciples of Jesus have been in furious squalls before, only to learn that their Savior can bring calm with his words, "Quiet! Be still!" (Mark 4:37-41; Luke 8:23-25). In the days of his flesh "Jesus went through all the towns and villages . . . healing every disease and sickness" (Matt. 9:35). Surely he, today, can heal the division and sickness of his own spiritual body, the church. The Great Physician is available and "in him all things hold together" (Col. 1:17). The *great* paralysis afflicting the church needs to be diagnosed by the *Greater Physician and the greatest* perscription needs to be followed for the desired cure to follow. Jesus is "the way" to oneness, "the truth" that unifies and "the life" who creates the qualities that enable togetherness.

Under the guiding hand of our common Lord, let us search the Scripture together, seeking to learn the true nature of the unity it advocates and learn from the Bible who are God's chosen instruments to pursue and find that oneness (Introduction). We need early to ask if unity is clearly the Lord's Divine Will. Six affirmative answers in Scripture will remove all doubts of that (Part

11

One). It will be important next to recognize the Devil's Dividing Walls that have been erected between believers to separate them. What seemingly innocent, but extremely deceptive, bait has Satan used to keep Christians apart? Six lures that may still be attractive to some need to be seen for what they are (Part Two). At this point we will need to turn to the Bible's Directing Word for guidance to be able to distinguish the "essential" gospel that must never be compromised and the "indifferent" doctrines that must at no time be allowed to divide. Six guide-posts of Revelation will be followed here (Part Three). The final chapters consider the Church's Demanding Way for our reconciliation. Here, noting the high cost, we must both ask if it is worth the effort and if it is actually attainable (Part Four). The conclusion accepts, as the bottom line, that nothing short of Christ-likeness is prerequisite to fully manifesting the unity of the Spirit.

You are invited, amidst the many voices shouting "Lo here!" or "Lo there!," to "find out what pleases the Lord" (Eph. 5:10). We ask you to join the apostle Paul in vowing, "We are not trying to please men but God, who tests our hearts" (I Thess. 2:4). Resolve to reduce tensions between brethren where you live and vow never to contribute to another division in the ranks of Christ's family wherever you go. "Blessed are the peacemakers" (Matt. 5:9). Be blest in fulfilling your mission as a son of God.

Endnotes

1. Walter A. Elwell, Ed. (Grand Rapids: Baker Book House, 1984), p. 231.

2. (New York: Ballantine Books, 1986), p. 403.

3. *The Last Years: Journals 1853-1855*, Ronald Gregor Smith, editor and translator, (New York: Harper and Row, 1965), pp. 136-137).

4. All Scriptural quotations, unless otherwise noted, will be from the *New International Version*, (Grand Rapids: Zondervan Bible Publishers, 1973).

5. *One Body One Gospel One World*, (London: William Carling and Company, Ltd., 1958), p. 54.

*I*NTRODUCTION:

UNITY AND THE PERSONS OF INFLUENCE

There is a majesty about the subject of Christian unity. We sense the need to remove our sandals, aware that in this theme we are standing on holy ground. Often we wonder if we are the ones who should be dealing with the topic at all. Is not the search for church oneness the lot of the clergy rather than the common person in the pew? Should not such holy things be left in the hands of the Archbishop of Canterbury, the Pope of Roman Catholicism and the national heads of the cooperating Protestant bodies?

My study and experience leads me to the opposite conclusion. The key unit in unity is you. The key church in oneness of believers is not a denomination but the local congregation of which you are a part. The Bible speaks of Christians and congregations, but knows nothing of denominations. Please do not

13

be offended when I speak of your denomination, if you are in one, as unscriptural. Is it not plain to see that it is as easy to find "Sears and Roebuck" in your New Testament as it is to find "United Methodist" or "Church of England?"

We are reminded of the man who, noticing a young woman futilely backing in and out of a tight parking space, rushed to her aid. A few minutes later, thanks to the gentleman's directings, she was parked neatly in the space. The woman experessed her gratitude with a "Thank you very much, sir." But, then she added, "This was very nice of you, but I was not attempting to get in. I was trying to get out!" Some churchmen today, who have been working hard at getting out of denominationalism, are beginning to wonder if their "leaders" are not just helping them into a larger one.

That uneasiness has been evident among Disciples of Christ. Perry Epler Gresham, then president of Bethany College in West Virginia, in the 1959 Convention of Disciples addressed the assembly, "The genius of our Movement is a call to the people of Christ to unite rather than a call for sovereign denominations to federate." In the April 4, 1982 issue of the "Disciple" magazine, their well respected historian A.T. DeGroot showed concern for that brotherhood's forming into a denomination. His opening paragraph reads, "By becoming 'a church' — among many other 'churches' (denominations) — we have become precisely what we condemned in our prior history." His concluding remarks are, "How *do* we conceive the world church? Is it a collection of denominations? That is what we now seem to say. In one century the wheel of our thought has turned 180 degrees."[1]

Those who labor for union of denominations need to ask the question of the later W.R. Walker: "How many unscriptural units do you have to unite before you have a scriptural whole?" With all the high ideals and good intentions of the modern ecumenical movement, is the right goal union and are the right people involved? I attended an ecumenical gathering a few weeks ago in Honolulu. It had been written up on the religious page of the local

newspaper as a major ecumenical event in which eight congregations would share, including Roman Catholics. There were seven
of the eight clergymen gowned in white robes on the platform. I
was more impressed that such a highly advertised event drew no
more than a couple dozen people on a Sunday night, counting
the platform personnel. The people of the churches, on this and
too many other occasions, are little touched by their
headquarter's hand-me-down programs. Loyalty from the rank
and file can not be missing, if the division problem is to be vic-
toriously faced. Unity at the bottom level is where the power to
transform lies. When God's people in their local fellowship see
the sin in sectarianism and the beauty in brotherhood, then
something good will follow. Major *differences* are problems, but
the major *indifference* is the greatest problem of all.

The Importance of You

Let me write a sentence of ten two letter words for you to
ponder: "If it is to be, it is up to me." Memorize these words. Affirm them again and again. Then apply them. This sentence can
solve the division problem before Rome and Canterbury can. The
word "unity" begins with "U." We are not to wait for something to
happen at some "upper level" conference and at some later time.
It is the "local level" where you live now that the Bible addresses.
At the "grass roots" in Corinth, Paul set out to meet the issue
before us. He wrote:

> I appeal to you, brothers, in the name of our Lord Jesus Christ,
> that all of you agree with one another so that there may be no
> divisions among you and that you may be perfectly united in mind
> and thought (I Cor. 1:10).

The letter was addressed "to those sanctified in Christ
Jesus . . . together with all those everywhere who call on the
name of our Lord Jesus Christ — their Lord and ours" (1:2).

15

In the Corinthian letter there was no admonition to wait for world leaders to discuss, agree and vote. Rather, each believer was to do what the Lord asked and to do it without tarrying. Church unity was not an administrative matter to be worked out by professionals over the heads of the people. The advocated oneness was each believer's responsibility under Christ's Lordship. As Barton W. Stone advocated so long ago, "Let every Christian begin the work of union in himself." The unity the Bible teaches is from the bottom up and not the top down. It is at that level every member squelches "division in the body" by having "equal concern for each other" (I Cor. 12:25).

No merger of any kind is a substitute for individual responsibility. When an apostle writes, "Make every effort to keep the unity of the Spirit through the bond of peace" (Eph. 4:3), he is expecting all readers to act and act now. The full energy of each saint is to be joined to that of the others to attain the unity goal. When a call rings out for harmony, it is at once an individual obligation to respond. Relationships between individuals and groups in the same congregation is where oneness is first to begin. And even when a letter is addressed to a church in Ephesus, Laodicea or Sardis, no member is to avoid its demand as if it was not to him, for "He who has an ear" is to respond to what "the Spirit says to the churches" (Rev. 2:7,11,17,29; 3:6,13,22).

The words of the New Testament, "Make every effort to keep the unity of the Spirit through the bond of peace" (Eph. 4:3), demand effort on the part of each hearer. God is not releasing any Christian from his responsibility to make contribution toward unity by sloughing the work onto the shoulders of a seminary-trained professional. The parties involved in concord are three — Christ, you and me. Our relation with Jesus is what relates us to one another. The ground of our unity is personal. The problem of discord will not be solved in some religious headquarters, but in your heart and mine.

The living faith of the so called "little people," is the answer to our schism. The Catholic theologian, Hans Kung, exalts the common man in Christ as the preserver of true Christianity in times when what passed as the church reflected against the truth. He observes:

> There were times when little of the truth of the gospel could be observed in the lives of hierarchs and theologians. . . . But when popes and bishops pursued power, money, and pleasure, and theologians kept silent, slept, produced apologias, or even collaborated, there still remained those innumerable, mostly unknown Christians . . . who tried even at the worst times of the Church to live according to the gospel.[2]

The fear is often expressed that common people going to the Bible, independent of the priesthood or clergy, would lead to confusion and certain division. The assumption behind the uneasiness is that Mr. and Mrs. Average Person cannot possibly understand Scripture, for it is beyond the grasp of people unless they are college graduates majoring in religious studies. We must not overlook that in Jesus' day "the common people heard him gladly" (Mark 12:37 KJV). Common people, to this day, read their Bible that they love and they follow it as God's Word to them. They find comfort in knowing that "everything that was written in the past was written to teach us, so that through endurance and the encouragement of the Scriptures we might have hope" (Rom. 15:4). It is that Scriptural knowledge that keeps many of them from following institutional leaders that would lead to paths uncharted in God's revelation. Christ's

> . . . sheep follow him because they know his voice . . . they will never follow a stranger; in fact, they will run away from him because they do not recognize a stranger's voice (John 10:4-5).

Common people, using common sense, can come to a common mind.

Believe in God. Also believe in yourself as an instrument He can use to bring harmony out of the discord amongst church people. You pose the question, "But what can one person do?" It is true that you can't do everything, but you can do something. You determine to be a Christian in the full sense of the word and vow never to become a partisan. And when some Euodia or Syntyche are in disagreement in your community, as in Paul's time they lived at Philippi, "I ask you (as a) loyal yokefellow (to) help these women" find unity again (Phil. 4:2-3). The next question after "What can I do?" is "What can my local congregation do?"

The Importance of Your Local Congregation

People power is beyond measuring. That means you are important and potent in bringing God's family together. People like you constitute the membership lists of the local churches across the world. What potential for change! Would you believe, while sitting in the grandstands at a world-series game, that "on any given Sunday there are probably more people in churches than the total number of people who attend professional sports events in a whole year?"[3] Think of the outcome if each local congregation would seek to be true in doctrine, holy in life and unifying in relationships. The power to conquer the evil of sectarianism is in "all the churches (congregations) of Christ" (Rom. 16:16). It is to these units in the Lord's army that the promise comes, "The God of peace will soon crush Satan under your feet" (Rom. 16:20).

Look at the church through God's eyes and you see but local congregations and the church universal, with nothing in between, such as denominational institutions. The New Testament knows of congregations in different places, but not of different types divided over structural formations. There were "churches in Galatia" (Gal. 1:2; I Cor. 16:1), "churches in the province of Asia" (I Cor. 16:19), "Macedonian churches" (II Cor. 8:1) and "churches of Judea" (Gal. 1:22). Only geography divided them. Denominational subdivisions in each town such as Colossae, Ephesus and Laodicea were not layered upon the territorial ones.

Rather their unity in Christ was expressed by letters, by gifts, and by visits. Mutual aid, gathering for worship and observing the Lord's supper bond a local membership together. Hearing the same apostles' teaching and praying for one another created a sense of oneness even among persons who never saw each other face to face.

When a letter to believers came revealing, "I hear that when you come together as a church, there are divisions among you" (I Cor. 11:18), the writer was not making reference to a problem between congregations but to a rift within a single community. That was where the difficulty existed and where it was to be solved.

In the local, gathered church of faithful persons Christ expected his authority to be recognized and his will fulfilled. Each individual worshiper, calling Jesus Lord, was to bend his will in loving obedience. Each single congregation was expected to show allegiance to its Master with no interference from outside sources.

All attempts at unity, if they would end in success and not failure, must study Scripture to learn the nature of the church. How does the Bible use the word "church"? The Greek ἐκκλησία means called-out ones. Of its 115 instances, around 96 times it has reference to a specific congregation in a particular locale. In no instance would the word church be used correctly of a lady's or men's group within a congregation or a denominational structure made up of several of such local entities. When Jesus speaks, "I will build my church" (Matt. 16:18), or Paul writes, "Christ loved the church and gave himself up for her" (Eph. 5:25), the singular "church" refers to the universal church made up of all the redeemed of every time and place. In this sense the Nicene Creed confesses faith in the "One Holy Catholic and Apostolic Church" (εἰς μίαν ἁγίαν καθολικὴν καὶ ἀποστολικὴν ἐκκλησίαν). The universal church — the whole church — refers to Christ's followers both militant and triumphant. The local church, where Christ's gospel is proclaimed and his supper and baptism observed, is a microcosm of the "una sancta." Theologians rightly

19

speak of the essence of the whole being present in each congregation of the faithful.

Robert Banks words it, "Each of the various local churches are tangible expressions of the heavenly church, manifestations in time and space of that which is essentially eternal and infinite in character."[4] In a similar vein J. Robert Nelson affirms, "It is perfectly clear according to the Bible the Church exists on two levels only. There is the one Church Universal on earth and in heaven. And there is the local congregation which is the focal point of the Church." To make his view unmistakably clear, he goes on, "In between there are no communions or denominations. . . . The New Testament has a very definite word for denominations. It addresses them negatively and in judgment. It calls into question their right to exist as separate and divided bodies."[5]

In strong opposition to this concept Charles Clayton Morrison in his book *The Unfinished Reformation* calls the congregational principle "an obstacle that must be surmounted in preparation for a united church." He considers it "quite unthinkable that any part of the church should set itself up as absolutely independent and autonomous" and calls "the theory of unqualified congregational independence and autonomy . . . incompatible with the ecumenical ideal."[6] Free churches rather sense their dependence on all who have gone before them and all who live beside them. They simply insist that joining denomination to denomination for the sake of structured union is not to be preferred to the voluntary fellowship of free people in Christ. When a congregation determines to be one of Christ's churches plus nothing, minus nothing and divided by nothing, it exhibits the Christian unity that is God given.

Donald F. Durnbaugh defines the "Believers' Church" as "the covenanted and disciplined community of those walking in the way of Jesus Christ. Where two or three such are gathered, willing also to be scattered in the work of their Lord, there is the believing people."[7]

Congregations free to choose their own affiliations are termed "free churches" in contradiction to persons obligated to accept commitments made by the actions of others. It is very possible that the ones who could do the most toward manifesting the unity Christ has given his people are not those who speak most loudly about it, nor attend national gatherings considering the topic, but those who have the attitude of love and acceptance that shows in all inter-personal and inter-congregational relationships.

If unity is to be visible, it is most apt to be seeable in a church locale where brotherhood is sensed and love overflows. Bible study led John Locke to this perception:

> A church . . . I take to be a voluntary society of men joining themselves together of their own accord in order to the public worshipping of God in such a manner as they judge acceptable to Him, and effectual to the salvation of their souls.
>
> I say it is a free and voluntary society. Nobody is born a member of any church. . . . No man by nature is bound unto any particular church or sect, but everyone joins himself voluntarily to that society in which he believes he has found that profession and worship which is truly acceptable to God."[8]

The only way the church can function is on the local level. In the local congregation there is opportunity for the "the apostles' teaching . . . fellowship . . . breaking of bread and . . . prayer" (Acts 2:42). There deacons can be chosen for service (Acts 6:3) and missionaries commissioned for foreign fields (Acts 13:2-3). There discipline can be applied (I Cor. 5:4-5) and needs of members be met by shepherds who know and care (Acts 20:28).

In every congregation where Christ alone is Lord, no one need change his or her church-membership to another congregation in the same area; for, at any point of deficiency, the church is free to change to apostolic standards. If that were not true, the New Testament epistles would not have been written. Each of these letters was written to individuals or to congregations. The recipients were to hear and then heed. Information resulted in

21

transformation then and can do the same now. A recipe found and followed will show the same ingredients put together in the same manner bringing the same results. The locus of transformation is the Christian's heart and the body of believers to which he is in covenant.

In the great Negro Spiritual, based on the children of Jehovah's conquest of Canaan, the victory line is, "When Joshua fit de battle of Jericho — The walls come tumblin' down." How soon will Christ's battle against sectarianism find the barriers crumbling? When the country boy responded to the tourist's question regarding the distance to a certain town, he said, "Your destination is 24,996 miles the way you are going, but if you'll turn around it ain't but four." To go the denominational merger route to unity may take forever. The best scenario on that road is but a larger denomination. But bigger and better sects, even though fewer in number, can not be the final vision of Christian unity. Such a creation would be evangelistically ineffective and Biblically incongruent. However, with local churches acting responsively, both here and now, the goal of scriptural oneness is attainable in a reasonable time. The question, "Am I my brother's keeper?" (Gen. 4:9) must only be answered with a strong, "Amen!"

Endnotes

1. P. 20-21.
2. *The Church: Maintained in Truth*, (New York: The Seabury Press, 1980), p. 31.
3. Peter L. Berger and Richard John Newhaus *To Empower People*, (Washington, D.C.: American Enterprise Institute for Public Policy Research, 1977), p. 27.
4. *Paul's Idea of Community: The Early House Churches in Their Historical Setting*, (Grand Rapids, Michigan: Eerdmans, 1980), p. 47.
5. *One Lord, One Church*, (New York: Associated Press, 1958), pp. 23-24.
6. P. 174ff.
7. *The Believer's Church*, (New York: The Macmillan Company, 1968), p. 33.

8. *Treatise of Civil Government and a Letter Concerning Toleration*, edited by Charles L. Sherman, (New York: Appelton-Century-Crifts, Inc., 1937), p. 175.

PART ONE

**THE LORD'S DIVINE WILL
FOR OUR ONENESS**

1

UNITY AND THE PLAINNESS OF THE SCRIPTURE

Since some persons still challenge the idea that unity is a desirable, we must examine the Scripture to see what is true (cp. Acts 17:11). Thomas Campbell in his Declaration and Address stated that:

> The church of Christ upon earth is essentially, intentionally and constitutionally one; consisting of all those in every place that profess their faith in Christ and obedience to Him in all things according to the Scriptures, and that manifest the same by their tempers and conduct.

Does the Bible agree that unity belongs to the *essence* of God's church and is in no way an insignificant side issue? Is the New Testament in agreement that Jesus deliberately *intended* the church to manifest unity, seeing division as rebellion against his will? Can the Scripture be counted on to support the idea that the

Lord *constituted* the church to be one and has revealed sufficiently clear marks by which it can be recognized and measured?

THE OLD TESTAMENT

The Jewish Confession of Faith, uttered twice a day by every adult male Jew and quoted as the first act of worship in every Jewish synagogue, is, "Hear, O Israel: The LORD your God, the Lord is one. Love the Lord your God with all your heart and with all your soul and with all your strength" (Deut. 6:4-5). Like the first commandment of the Decalogue, this creed is a monotheistic declaration that there is but one God, unique and supreme. The "Shemah" (so called because it is the opening Hebrew word of the declaration) is not offering Israel a pantheon of deities around each of which sects of worshipers can cluster. One God affirms one people of God.

Throughout Israel's Bible are commendations of unity and condemnations of division. Each person in covenant with God is to "Pray for the peace of Jerusalem," interceding, "May there be peace within your walls" (Psalm 122:6-7). Each worshiper is to "seek peace and pursue it" (Psalm 34:14). All readers of Old Covenant Scriptures are to hear the order: "This is what the LORD says: Do not go up to fight against your brothers" (II Chron. 11:4). No Israelite is to miss the constant wisdom of Proverbs that, page after page, warns against division. In this book of wise sayings it is evident that "There are six things the LORD hates, seven that are detestable to him" and the climax of the list is "a man who stirs up dissension among brothers" (6:16,19). Let each young Jew remember, "Better a dry crust with peace and quiet than a house full of feasting, with strife" (17:1). The counsel is, "Starting a quarrel is like breaching a dam; so drop the matter before a dispute breaks out" (17:14). Let a spade be called a spade. Let evil be seen for what it is. "He who loves a quarrel loves sin; he who builds a high gate invites destruction" (17:19). The man who causes fusses locks the door against future amity, in that "disputes are like the barred gates of a citadel" (18:19). The better way, when emotions of anger overtake you, is to quickly "clap your hand over your mouth! For as churning the milk produces butter, and as twisting the nose produces blood, so stirring up anger produces strife" (30:32-33).

The hand-writing on the wall in Belshazzar's day (Mene, Mene, Tekel, Parsin) predicted that Babylon's days were numbered and that the kingdom divided would be given to others (Daniel 5:26-28). When division hits at any time or place, that community's days are numbered as well. Death, division and destruction follow. Yet, the prophets not only predicted the bad-news of division, they foretold the coming "Prince of Peace" (Isa. 9:6) and the wonderful Christian era when God promises, "I will pour out my Spirit on all people" (Joel 2:28-29). In that day sexual divisions will fade away as together "sons and daughters will prophesy" and "both men and women" will receive God's Spirit." Age distinctions will lose significance as "old men will dream dreams" and "young men will see visions" all in the same family of God. In the Ancient Prophets we see destruction was left behind as armies of locusts came across a land, because in unity "They do not jostle each other; each marches straight ahead. They plunge through defenses without breaking ranks" (Joel 2:8). But, in those same writings we learn that blessing will be the consequences in the world, when God's missionary church marches in unison with its saving gospel.

The preacher (Ecclesiastes) proclaims: "Two are better than one." His reasoning is:

> If one falls down, his friend can help him up. But pity the man who falls and has no one to help him up! Also, if two lie down together, they will keep warm. But how can one keep warm alone? Though one may be overpowered, two can defend themselves. A cord of three strands is not quickly broken (Eccl. 4:9-12).

Solomon in all his wisdom is arguing for unity, harmony and

oneness. He, and other wisemen, saw that careless words could harm irreparably but that "the tongue that brings healing is a tree of life" (Prov. 15:4). Yet, Solomon's father, David, gave us the most beautiful of all testimonies to the beauty of harmony. Listen to his Psalm 133:

> How good and pleasant it is when brothers live together in unity! It is like precious oil poured on the head, running down on the beard, running down on Aaron's beard, down upon the collar of his robes. It is as if the dew of Hermon were falling on Mount Zion. For there the LORD bestows his blessing (vv. 1-3).

This magnificent Psalm is beautifully structured. The first verse is the opening affirmation, followed by two metaphors comparing unity first to precious oil and then to refreshing dew. Although the psalm is short, it contains a magnanimous truth. Unity is the desired state to be enjoyed by brothers, who are brothers because they are in God's family. The Psalm is labeled "a song of ascents," because on those annual occasions, when Jews scattered across the world returned to worship at their Jerusalem temple, they could join in singing of their family ties as their caravan ascended up the mountains toward their temple. Passover, Pentecost and Tabernacles were festivals that drew the dispersed nation together and renewed their brotherly relations as God's people.

Each singer knew that while some "good things" are not "pleasant" and some "pleasant" things are not "good," unity is both "good and pleasant." On the basis of this truth, we can teach that unity has all the blessings of a family reunion. On the awareness of this fact, we can understand what the Father in the Prodigal Son story wanted for both his sons (Luke 15:11-32). In the KJV of Psalm 133, the opening word calls for eyes to "behold" the beauty of oneness. In Jesus' story of the prodigal's unbrotherly brother, we "behold" the ugliness of division in God's family, rather than the desired "good" and "pleasant" oneness. Verse two illustrates the "good" aspect of unity and verse three the "pleasant" side of that oneness.

In the Psalm writer's mind is not just any high priest, but Aaron (Lev. 8:1-13). The oil of anointing was "precious," containing the ingredients of myrrh, cinnamon, cane, cassia and olive (cp. Exodus 30:23-25). This sweet-scented oil compounded with aromatic spices, while intended for the head (Exodus 29:7), was not confined to it (Exodus 29:21, cp. Mark 14:3-4,9; Luke 7:46). In Aaron's case the oil ran beyond his head, over his beard, even on to "the collar of his robes." The "collar" was the hole in the garment through which the head was to pass. The Hebrew word literally means the "mouth," "opening" or "neckline" (cp. Exod. 28:32). Some commentators visualize the profusely poured oil flowing beyond head, beard and collar all the way to the skirt of the High Priest's robe. The point is that brotherly unity is not to be sparingly sprinkled, but is to extravagantly and abundantly flow out to all. Did not a High Priest wear the breastplate, bearing the names of all twelve tribes? That testimony and symbol of Israel's unity was under the "trickle down" effect of God's Spirit. Heaven's good will cannot be confined to but one spot. Love's aroma and fragrance is to be enjoyed by all around.

Unity's second parallel in this song is that of dew. Just as oil flows down, so does dew descend with its refreshment. It is from above that unity flows to the people. "Hermon," the highest mountain in Israel, is at the far North of the nation and "Zion," little by comparison, is to the South. The Jordan, Palestine's one great river, flows from the melting snows and descending dew of Hermon, bringing moisture and fertility to the fields below. Travelers report that the excessive dew of Hermon is so abundant that mornings look as if it had rained all night.

Unity is said to be God's refreshing dew from on high that is meant to blanket with its blessing, every believer from North to South (cp. Hosea 14:5). It is not of man's devising. Harmony descends from heaven as God's gift. "The LORD bestows his blessing, even life forever more" (Psa. 133:3).

THE NEW TESTAMENT

To read the Old Testament on the unity theme is to find that the Scripure is plain in advocating the oneness of the family of God. How about the New? Let us, now, just sample a few of the unity texts in the New Covenant Scriptures. In the Gospels Jesus speaks of his sheep being "one flock and one shepherd" (John 10:16) and the Apostle John interprets the words of the High Priest Caiaphas, regarding Jesus' death, being "not only for the nation but also for the scattered children of God, to bring them together and make them one" (John 1:52). In the Synoptic Gospels Jesus gives the teaching that "Every kingdom divided against itself will be ruined, and every city or household divided against itself will not stand" (Matt. 12:25 cp. Mark 3:24-25; Luke 11:17). In my imagination I visualize all hell breaking loose in rejoicing at these words, for the only way Satan's forces could ever destroy the church had been uncovered. To divide Christians would be to conquer his kingdom, for divided — like any city, household or kingdom — it would fall. Satan has been working at that objective from the day the church was founded. Over those same centuries the Lord has been teaching his followers to think of their belonging together, by praying "Our Father . . . our daily bread . . . our debts" and not the individualistic "my" and "mine" (Matt. 6:9-12). In Matthew's gospel Jesus predicts that on the truth of his sonship, "I will build my church" (16:18). No hint is given of a plurality of denominations claiming to be all or part of that church.

Luke's historical record of the early church tells how the kingdom began on a Pentecost when "they were all together in one place" (Acts 2:1). The converts so "devoted themselves . . . to the fellowship" (2:42) that "all the believers were together and had everything in common" (2:44). "They continued to meet together" and eat "together" (2:46). In Jerusalem it could be said, "All the believers were one in heart and in mind" (4:32). One place for their common assembly in

32

that city was Solomon's Colonnade, where "all the believers used to meet together" (5:12).

In the book of Acts three little words make one great case against believers being walled off from one another. Consider the pronoun "we," the conjunction "and" and preposition "with." "We" speaks of persons together. Acts 16:10 (KJV) reads, "after he had seen the vision, immediately we endeavored to go." New Testament scholars often speak of the "we sections" of Acts (16:10-18; 20:5-21:26; 27:1-28:16), referring to the places where Luke, the author of the book, is with the missionary Paul in the work of planting churches. Let the plural pronoun also speak of the believers working together, suffering together, worshipping together and laboring together in the cause of the gospel. Also, be impressed by the conjunction "and," as Luke writes, for instance, of "Paul and Barnabas" (11:30; 12:25; 13:2,50; 15:2), "Paul and Silas" (16:19,25,29; 17:4), "Peter and John" (3:1,11; 4:13; 8:14), "Priscilla and Aquila" (18:2,26). People teamed together to do the work of evangelism. Or, follow the preposition "with." In the upper-room the apostles were there, but they were not alone. "They all joined together constantly in prayer . . . with the women and Mary the mother of Jesus and with his brothers" (1:14). As Peter preached on the first day of the church, he is not alone on his feet; rather "Peter stood up with the Eleven" (2:14). And so the work goes on with people standing shoulder to shoulder, marching side by side, in their Master's bidding.

The epistles crescendo with the same praise of, and call for, unity. The author of Hebrews calls on his Jewish-Christian brothers to "not give up meeting together" but to "encourage one another" (10:25). His plea is that they make every effort to live in peace" (12:14) and that they "keep on loving each other as brothers" (13:1). Simon Peter summons his readers, "Finally, all of you, live in harmony with one another; be sympathetic as brothers" (I Pet. 3:8). He commands them to "seek peace and pursue it" (I Pet. 3:11) and he gives the greeting consistent with such an order, "Peace to all of you who are in Christ" (I Pet.

5:14). Jude is ever "very eager to write . . . about the salvation we share" (v. 3) and John is ever ready to conceive of the church as "those who reverence (God's) name, both small and great" (Rev. 11:18).

These voices for Christian unity are but background music for the lead soloist Paul. In his earliest writings to the Galatians and Thessalonians, his voice echoes from the rafters, as he condemns division. He lists "the acts of the sinful nature" and places at the center "hatred, discord, jealousy, fits of rage, selfish ambition, dissensions (and) factions" (Gal. 5:19-20). With the vibrato of a trembling heart he warns, "If you keep on biting and devouring each other, watch out or you will be destroyed by each other" (Gal. 5:15). The soft tones of affection are heard, as in joy at good-news, he sings out the praise, "the love every one of you has for each other is increasing" (II Thess. 1:3). This joy followed his earlier encouragement, "Live in peace with each other" (I Thess. 5:13) and "greet all the brothers with a holy kiss" (5:26). No higher note in the song of unity is struck than when the Apostle to the Gentiles chants:

> You are all sons of God through faith in Christ Jesus, for all of you who were baptized into Christ have clothed yourself with Christ. There is neither Jew or Greek, slave nor free, male nor female, for you are all one in Christ Jesus. If you belong to Christ, then you are Abraham's seed, and heirs according to the promise (Gal. 3:26-29).

The range of Paul's musical score reached this high note, only after the lowest note in his memory, when Peter "began to draw back and separate himself from the Gentiles . . . not acting in line with the truth of the gospel" (Gal. 2:12-14).

The Prison Epistles sing the same song of unity as God's will "to bring all things in heaven and on earth together under one head, even Christ" (Eph. 1:10). The Gentiles once "separate" and "excluded" are now "brought near through the blood of Christ" (Eph. 2:12-13). Christ "our peace . . . has made the two one and has destroyed the barrier, the dividing wall of hostility"

(Eph. 2:14). That is something to sing about. Former aliens and foreigners are now "fellow citizens with God's people and members of God's household . . . built together to become a dwelling in which God lives by his Spirit" (Eph. 2:19-22). Such a glorious truth sets our hearts to joining in the words of thanksgiving. As Gentiles become "heirs together with Israel, members together of one body, and sharers together in the promise in Christ Jesus" (Eph. 3:6), who can not but join in to the hallelujah chorus of gratitude. We have a "gospel of peace" (Eph. 6:15) that produces a "love . . . for all the saints" (Col. 1:4) and makes the heart desire to "greet all the saints" (Phil. 4:21), leaving not one person out. It is the constant prayer of God's leaders that a congregation "stand firm in one spirit, contending as one man for the faith of the gospel" (Phil. 1:27).

The Pauline Pastorals keep affirming the same goodness of unity, calling Titus his "true son in our common faith" (Titus 1:4) and admonishing Timothy to see that the church leaders everywhere be men who "lift up holy hands in prayer without anger or disputing" (I Tim. 2:8). What is to be shunned completely are "foolish and stupid arguments, because . . . they produce quarrels" (II Tim. 2:23). Quarrels are "unprofitable and useless." A divisive person deserves only two clear warnings. "After that," the evangelist is to "have nothing to do with him" (Titus 3:9-10).

The heavy theological writing, which is Romans, seeks for the believers to "live in harmony with one another" (12:16), and to "make every effort to do what leads to peace and to mutual edification" (14:19). It contains the prayer, "May the God who gives endurance and encouragement give you a spirit of unity among yourselves as you follow Christ Jesus, so that with one heart and mouth you may glorify the God and Father of our Lord Jesus Christ." The book of Romans admonishes the hearers to "accept one another, then, just as Christ accepted you, in order to bring praise to God" (15:5-7).

The Corinthian correspondence reflects Paul's "fear that there may be quarreling, jealousy, outbursts of anger (and) factions" (II

35

Cor. 12:20), where there should have been "one mind" and "peace" (13:11). The God of the Bible "is not a God of disorder but of peace" (I Cor. 14:33) and he "has called us to live in peace" (I Cor. 7:15).

In the first Corinthian letter, written in 55 AD, the apostle gives the first four chapters to the problem of division in that local assembly. Put your ear close to the passage and you can almost hear the heart-beat of the great man of God who founded that congregation. He writes:

> I appeal to you, brothers, in the name of our Lord Jesus Christ, that all of you agree with one another so that there may be no divisions among you and that you may be perfectly united in mind and thought. My brothers, some from Chloe's household have informed me that there are quarrels among you. What I mean is this: One of you says, "I follow Paul"; another, "I follow Apollos"; another, "I follow Cephas"; still another, "I follow Christ." Is Christ divided? Was Paul crucified for you? Were you baptized into the name of Paul? (1:10-13).

The I Corinthian letter deals with many problems in that local body of believers, but first on the list — because prime in importance — is the disunity manifesting itself there. Paul labels it σχίσματα or dissension. A σχίσμα is a rip or tear, as in a garment. There were "quarrels" between the members. These ἔριδες were hot disputes as the result of intolerable rivalry fed by the flames of uncontrolled emotion. The need of the hour was for the membership to be "united" ("joined" KJV) or "knit together." Here Paul uses a medical term used often in describing the joining of fractured bones. There needed to be the restoring of Christ's body to its rightful condition of togetherness. N.B. Hardeman, in Volume 3 of his *Tabernacle Sermons*, teaches that if the bone of the arm were to be knit together that would be unity, since elements of the same kind would be blended together in a cohesive manner. But, when skin attaches to another organ, it forms an adhesion. That is a case of blending elements of different kinds. Hardeman's interest was to show the difference between church union and

Christian unity.

You may have noticed that the name of Jesus had been used by Paul nine times in the opening nine verses in his first Corinthian letter. Christ's name is the antithesis of division and the "appeal" to harmony. For Jesus' sake, let his followers drop their party cries and their over-exaltation of certain of the Lord's "servants" (3:5), and let them remember who was "crucified" for them and into whom they were "baptized" (1:13). New Testament writers use the Spirit-guided phrase "in Christ" 254 times, but never "in Augustine, in Luther, in Calvin, in Wesley, etc., etc." Appreciation of Jesus' servants is always appropriate and is to be encouraged. But, lifting any one of the Lord's workers to the position of party-leader is never proper and to be condemned. Our oath of allegiance was made to Christ in our baptism, not to one of his workers. The last line by Paul, before entering the lengthy condemnation of division in the ranks (1:10-4:21), reminds each hearer "God . . . called you into fellowship with his Son Jesus Christ" (1:9). That fellowship is too precious to be destroyed by division.

As we scan the New Testament to find the "Lord's Divine Will" on the topic of unity, we are seeking to find if the Scripture is plain in its teaching on the matter. Everyone can agree that I Corinthians is plain indeed. Yet, before we conclude this overview, Ephesians 4 demands attention, as it pleads for "the unity of the Spirit" (4:3). The phrase "unity of the Spirit" is not a genitive of possession but a genitive of originating cause. The unity described here is a unity of which God's Spirit is the author. If American democracy in Abraham Lincoln's words is a "government of the people, by the people and for the people," Christian unity in Paul's thought is the "government of God, by God and for God."

One is not surprised to find mention of the "one . . . Father" (v. 6), "one Lord" (4:5) and "one Spirit" (4:4) in chapter 4, having shared in the trinitarian doxology of chapter 1, where there is praise of the Father (1:3-6), the Son (1:7-12) and the Spirit (1:13-14) for our redemption. The God-given unity described is in one sense to be *maintained*, and yet in another sense is to be *attained*. By virtue of the gift of salvation we are made one body. The elements of that oneness are "one body and one Spirit . . . one hope . . . one Lord, one faith, one baptism; one God and Father of all" (4:4-6). This unity, which is ours because we are in Christ is to be preserved at all cost. Each participant is to "make every effort to keep" it (4:3). NEB uses the words "spare no effort." That is the duty — the present duty — of all of us. But the "now" of our oneness is anticipating the "not yet," when one day "we all reach unity in the faith and in the knowledge of the Son of God and become mature, attaining to the whole measure of the fulness of Christ" (4:13).

The essential attitude preceding the manifestation of our oneness is expressed in the words, "Be completely humble and gentle; be patient, bearing with one another in love" (4:2). In other words, "the fruit of the Spirit" (Gal. 5:22-23) and the "unity of the Spirit" go together. Behavior and status are joined. So are "one body and one Spirit," for the church body without the Spirit's animation would be a dead body. United also are "one faith" and "one baptism," for without this sequence baptism would be an empty rite (cp. Mark 16:16; Acts 8:12; 16:14-15, 31-33), rather than the grand confession of faith that it is.

We must conclude that the unity of the Spirit is more than having a spirit of congeniality, as important as that is. The "unity of the Spirit" is shared in by only those who are indwelt by God's Spirit upon their obedience to the gospel (Acts 5:32). The rest do "not belong to Christ" (Rom. 5:5).

The "unity in the faith" (4:13) is based on the revelation given by the Spirit of truth. No union, with less than Christ as the head, his word as the rule and conformity to that truth the terms, can be the desired unity of the Spirit. When God speaks there must be conformity or rebellion, and rebellion is never unity. One may leave God's basis, but the basis stands unchanged. There is but "one body," into which "we were all baptized by one Spirit" (I Cor. 12:13) and so we share equally with all other Christians in the "one hope." There is unity of authority in the "one Lord," unity of message in the "one faith," and unity of worship toward the "one God."

On the basis of this unifying doctrine all Christians are to share in the unifying work of ministration. For these "works of service" (4:12) each individual has been given an endowment or gift (χάρισμα). The same Spirit has given to us a diversity of abilities that, by coordination of the Head, each member cooperatively can share in God's service in perfect unity without uniformity.

For the benefit of each one of us and to prepare for this united service, the ascended Lord (4:8-11) by means of the Spirit sent functionaries into the church to minister in the Word. There were given "apostles" and "prophets" to reveal and confirm the teaching, "evangelists" to proclaim it and "pastors and teachers" to build up disciples by it to the point that they can function effectively for God.

This Bible unity can not be equated to convention attendance, agency support or organizational cooperation. Men can manipulate organizations but they can not change the eternal Spirit. Divinely revealed unity is something we are to "make every effort to keep" (4:3), in each locality and in every life indwelt by the Spirit, by letting the Spirit of holiness and truth possess it. Even a cursory reading of Ephesians 4, I Corinthians 1, Psalm 133 or the many other texts suggested lead to the conclusion — unity? Yes! Division? Never!

2

UNITY AND THE PICTURES OF THE CHURCH

The Bible is abundant in texts that extol unity and pronounce judgment on division. God's Book is also rich in descriptions of the Church that demand oneness. In the New Testament Christ's church is compared to a body, a bride, a family, etc. — 95 different ways in all. Yet, in each way to view the church, the imagery demands unity. You get the correct idea from these analogies that one cannot be a Christian by oneself. Christianity, while very personal is not private. To say that it is personal is to speak of it as relational. Those in covenant with Christ are by that fact in relationship to all others in him. There is in Scripture God's "Yea and Amen" to the concept of community and covenant relations. Yet there is His "Nay" to an experiential dimension that ties you to Jesus above you but, in no way, connects you to brothers beside you. "A good soldier of Jesus Christ" (II Tim. 2:3), that will "fight the good fight" (I Tim. 1:8), clad in "the full armor of God" (Eph. 6:13) and equipped with "weapons" able to "demolish strongholds" (II Cor. 10:4), knows that he is in God's army and does not march alone. Rabbi and disciples, King and people, vine and branches or shepherd and flock all speak of togetherness.

Like Old Testament Israel (Ezek. 34:12), the church is God's flock with Christ as chief shepherd (Heb. 13:20) and elders as his under-shepherds (I Pet. 5:2; Acts 20:28). The sheep are many, but the flock is one (John 10:16). The branches are many, but the vine is one (John 15:1,5). The vinedresser is not busy uniting branch to branch, but he is concerned that each branch is connected to the vine for its sustenance and fruit-bearing. Because of that life-sustaining relationship to Christ the vine, all the branches see their oneness. No Bible text would lead a reader to think of denominations as branches of the church. The branches are the individual Christians who receive their strength from Jesus and produce fruit for him. W.H. Book, when asked what branch of the church he represented, gave the only Biblically consistent reply, answering, "I do not represent any branch at all. I represent the vine, and am a full-grown branch myself." Christ, the vine, can produce only Christians, as a watermelon vine can produce watermelons but not tomatoes or cucumbers.

Even the concept of the church as "God's building" (I Cor. 3:9) or "temple" (I Cor. 3:6, cp. II Cor. 6:16) sees the individuals bound together as "living stones," making "a spiritual house" (I Pet. 2:5). In Christ "the whole building is joined together to become a dwelling in which God lives by his Spirit" (Eph. 2:21-22). God never intended for a board to remain by itself or a brick to refuse being cemented to the other bricks. The late James Earl Ladd used to tell of a soap-box orator he heard in the open-air setting harangue: "God is alright and Christ is alright but to H____ with the church." The evangelist then made it plain that it is not conceivable that a person could be attached to the head and deny relationship to the body. To be "baptized . . . into one body" (I Cor. 12:13) is not a different experience than being "baptized into Christ Jesus" (Rom. 6:3). We must not think we can decapitate Jesus. The head and the body are forever connected. If you belong to Christ, you belong to the church. To ask, "Must I belong to the church to be saved?" is to inquire, "Must I belong to Jesus to be redeemed?" Individualism is out. Going it alone has no place. To say you have Christ but find no time for the church, is to know nothing of the Bible's portrayal.

THE BODY IMAGERY

Paul learned on the Damascus Road that, when he brought harm to any member of the church, Jesus could ask, "Why do you persecute me?" (Acts 26:14). Christ is so closely identified with the persons who make up his body the church that to "sin against . . . brothers" is to "sin against Christ" (I Cor. 8:12). The apostle used the body imagery in Romans (12:4-5), I Corinthians (12:12-27), Ephesians (1:23; 4:4,12,16,25), and Colossians (1:18; 2:19; 3:15).

To speak of Christ as the head of the body demands unity — one head for one body. Denominational thinking, where each religious body claims Christ as head, brings to mind a monstrosity of 200 bodies connected in some way to a single head. The New Testament picture is a beautiful one. It speaks of the intimacy of a believer's relationship to Christ, who is the head that controls the actions of every member of his body. This portrayal suggests the closeness of each member to all the others, for every organ functions not for itself but for the good of the whole. The responsibility of the body-parts is to carry out the will of "the head of the body" (Col. 1:18).

In the body of the church there are many parts but no parties. No "member" is in competition with any other member. Together every part is to work in harmony and cooperation. Paul never tires telling the Ephesians there is but "one body." He does so in 2:16; 3:6; 4:4 and 4:25. I like to visualize a body with Christ as the head, giving all the directions; the eyes as the elders, overseeing all the work; the mouth as the teachers and preachers, telling redemption's story, the hands as the deacons, rendering service to any in need and the feet as the callers, going into the community to contact the populace. The very heart of that body may be even the shut-ins who pray daily for its welfare and growth.

Somewhere (Aesop?) I heard the fable that one day it occurred to body members that they were doing all the work but the stomach was getting all the food. A meeting was held and the members decided to strike until the stomach did its share of the work. After a few days, while the hands, mouth and teeth, did not work, they got into a bad condition. Soon the hands could hardly move, the mouth became parched and the legs found it increasingly difficult to support the body. In time the other members of the body learned that the stomach had been doing its part after all. The moral was that all members must work together or the body would go to pieces. The Christian application could well be that every Christian in the ministry (i.e. the priesthood of all believers) is a healthier concept than the paralyzing idea that only "clergy" are ministers and the others sit to the side.

If you are a "member" of the church, you need to discover "what member" you are. Members of a body have a function to perform. Eyes and hands, or preachers and deacons, have different roles to fill. Let each of us find where we fit in the body and, finding our place, let us function well for the benefit of all the other members in that body.

THE FAMILY IMAGERY

The last five letters of the word community are unity. There is no more basic community on earth than the family. The family-ties are bonds of unity not to be broken. John in sadness speaks of some leaving the church. He bemoans, "They went out from us, but they did not really belong to us. For if they had belonged to us, they would have remained with us; but their going showed that none of them belonged to us" (I John 2:19). Is there any stronger image of church unity than the family image? Let us just sit back and listen to the aging John speak: "Anyone who claims

44

to be in the light but hates his brother is still in the darkness" (I John 2:9,11). "Anyone who does not do what is right is not a child of God; nor is anyone who does not love his brother" (I John 3:10). "We know that we have passed from death to life, because we love our brothers. Anyone who does not love remains in death. Anyone who hates his brother is a murderer, and you know that no murderer has eternal life in him" (I John 3:14-15). "Love . . . is how we know that we belong to the truth" (I John 3:18-19).

Today we sing, "I'm so glad I'm a part of the family of God." The strains of that song are as old as the church. In the first century believers knew they were "members of God's household" (Eph. 2:19, cp. Heb. 3:6), "sons of God . . . God's children . . . heirs" (Rom. 8:14-17, cp. Gal. 4:6-7). They looked toward their heavenly home in "the Spirit of sonship" to "cry, 'Abba, Father' " (Rom. 8:16). They would "kneel before the Father, from whom his whole family in heaven and on earth derives its name" (Eph. 3:14-15). They would "do good to all people, especially to those who belong to the family of believers" (Gal. 6:10).

This New Testament way of viewing the church does not see an institution but a people who belong to each other, because God is their common Father. Family members can neither be voted out nor voted in. The church is not a club where members can be dropped from the rolls because of spasmodic attendance. Wayward family members they may be; but, if born to the Father, in the family they are. Unity is enhanced when each child of God is aware of the whole household. Unity is furthered, when in dealing with the misbehaving children, we are "gentle . . . like a mother caring for her little children" or "as a father . . . encouraging, comforting and urging" (I Thess. 2:7,11-12, cp. 5:11). Given the family character of the early church, the house church was a natural. Meeting in the homes of members, the family atmosphere gave expression to the common bond of love.

It is easy to see why the term "brother" ("brethren" KJV)

45

became Paul's favorite and most common address for believers. "My brothers, you whom I love and long for" (Phil. 4:1), he wrote to the Philippians. "Holy and faithful brothers in Christ" (Col. 1:2), he addressed the Colossians. "If anyone does not obey your instruction . . . do not regard him as an enemy, but warn him as a brother" (II Thess. 3:14-15), he counselled Thessalonians. Paul's Old Testament Bible knew the concept of brotherhood. Its story of Abraham and Lot records the conversation, "Let's not have any quarreling between you and me, or between your herdsmen and mine, for we are brothers" (Gen. 13:8). Its prophet's counsel is, "Say of your brothers, 'My people,' and of your sisters, 'My loved ones.' " (Hosea 2:1). Its convicting questions are, "Have we not all one Father? Did not God create us? Why do we profane the covenant of our fathers by breaking faith with one another?" (Mal. 2:10). But, of even more impact on Paul than his Scriptures was his Savior. Jesus had spoken, "Whoever does the will of my Father in heaven is my brother and sister and mother" (Matt. 12:50, cp. Mark 3:35). The Teacher had described the final judgment's verdict as based on the treatment of those he called "these brothers of mine" (Matt. 25:40).

"Love the brotherhood of believers" (I Pet. 2:17), "your brothers throughout the world" (5:9) becomes an easier command to obey when we realize that each believer, like the other, has "been born again, not of perishable seed, but of imperishable, through the living and enduring word of God" (1:23). That brotherhood of twice-born persons is God-given family based on the grace of God. Brotherhood comes not from possessing the same religious views but from originating from the same Heavenly Father. I may choose to hold a certain millennial view, but I have no choice in picking a brother. As W. Carl Ketcherside so definitively wrote in his journal *Mission Messenger*:

> I can no more choose my spiritual brothers than I can my fleshly brothers. Brotherhood is established by fatherhood; fraternity is the result of paternity. I shall love all my brothers and move

46

among them as they will allow, sharing in what they can convey, sharing with them what little I have learned. I shall receive them as God received me, not because of perfection, but in spite of imperfection.[1]

The jovial Joe Dampier, when asked while teaching at Milligan College if descendants of the reformation stemming from such workers as Thomas and Alexander Campbell were a denomination or a brotherhood, shot back with his quick wit. He responded, "A denomination is held together by machinery and a brotherhood by religion. We do not have enough machinery to be a denomination, nor enough religion to be a brotherhood." I am confident that he would agree that anyone with ties to a Restoration Movement should be first to make movement toward restoring the full Bible meaning to the term "brotherhood" to include every member of God's grand family. To that family God promised, "I will be a Father to you, and you will be my sons and daughters, says the Lord Almighty" (II Cor. 6:18).

THE BRIDE IMAGERY

The photo album of Scripture, which pictures Christ's people as his body and his family, clearly commends Christian unity and harmonious relationships. So does the bride and groom illustration. No relationship is more intimate than marriage. No ceremony is more beautiful than that involving the wedding vows. No commitment is more important than that between a husband and his bride. And no tragedy is more disrupting than the breaking of the marriage covenant.

God says, "I hate divorce." To Him it is to "profane the covenant" and is "breaking faith with one another." In explanation as to why prayers are not heard, it is written, "It is because the LORD made them one. . . . And why one? Because he was seeking godly offspring" (Mal. 2:10-16).

The master-painting of married love, painted in words by Paul and meant to be hung in the hall of our memories, is on the canvas of Ephesians 5. Enjoy its rich colors and enrapturing shapes. View the mural as a whole before studying any brush strokes or shadings at any particular spot. Here it is, for your viewing:

> Submit to one another out of reverence for Christ. Wives, submit to your husbands as to the Lord. For the husband is the head of the wife as Christ is the head of the Church, his body, of which he is the Savior. Now as the church submits to Christ, so also wives should submit to their husbands in everything. Husbands, love your wives, just as Christ loved the church and gave himself up for her to make her holy, cleansing her by the washing with water through the word, and to present him to herself as a radiant church, without stain or wrinkle or any other blemish, but holy and blameless. In this same way, husbands ought to love their wives as their own bodies. He who loves his wife loves himself. . . . For this reason a man will leave his father and mother and be united to his wife, and the two will become one flesh. This is a profound mystery — but I am talking about Christ and the church (Eph. 5:21-32, cp. I Pet. 3:5).

Notice that the very next chapter and verse speaks of "children," for they are the fruit of married love. Perhaps you have noticed the same progression in the Gospel of Matthew. Jesus gives teaching on marriage in 19:1-12. The next act is the blessing of the little children in verses 13-15. It is the relationship of husband and wife that creates a relationship of these parents to family. Rather than side with Hillel or Shammai on the divisive divorce question, Jesus took his listeners to God's original design for marriage recorded in the first book of the Bible. " 'Haven't you read,' he replied, 'that at the beginning the Creator made them male and female,' and said, 'For this reason a man will leave his father and mother and be united to his wife, and the two will become one flesh'? So they are no longer two, but one" (Matt. 19:4-6, cp. Mark 10:7-9).

The bigamist or polygamist image is not the picture Christ

gave for his church. How can the world, looking at hundreds of denominations, see God's one lovely bride? You cannot have two or two-hundred brides and neither can the bridegroom Christ claim the varied, numerous sects as his own. Each Christian in relationship with all other Christians constitute the one bride, one temple, one flock, one body, one kingdom. In a family spat one day, when tempers began to flare, the husband brought the quarrel to a quick end. Remembering his wedding vows, he broke into the conversation. "Wait a minute! We are not going to get a divorce. We might as well learn to live happily together."

In an old sermon of mine, titled "The Divine Arithmetic of Marriage," two of my equations were $1 + 1 = 1$ and $1 - 1 = 2$. In the former point I simply followed Jesus' assertion that in marriage "the two will become one" (Matt. 19:5). And as the marriage ceremony reads, the couple will become "one in name, one in aim and one in happy destiny." My latter point of $1 - 1 = 2$ was to show that when one party is inconsiderate of the other and leaving out the other, they have become two again. There may be no legal divorce and they may live under the same roof, but the oneness is gone. What can happen in a home, can happen in a church. This once again illustrates the great difference between "union" and "unity." Two prisoners chained together are united in one way, but if they are enemies, there is no unity.

Endnotes

1. Volume 25, Number 4, April 1963, p. 54.

3

UNITY AND THE PROCLAMATION OF THE SUPPER

God's will for unity can be learned in the careful reading of Scripture. It can also be gained in the proper observance of the Lord's Supper. The apostles' teaching is that "whenever you eat this bread and drink this cup, you proclaim the Lord's death" (I Cor. 11:26), but not only that, you proclaim the oneness of Christ's church. How else can we understand Paul when he states, "Because there is one loaf, we, who are many, are one body, for we all partake of the one loaf" (10:17)?

Communion is an action that speaks louder than words. The action, accompanied by the words of institution and interpretation, makes the message clearer still. The passover meal, from the days of the Exodus out of Egypt to the upper-room in Jerusalem where Christ instituted the new supper for the Christian era, had its symbolic story to tell. Let's review that typological proclamation, before we hear the testimony of the Lord's table to unity.

The annual passover Seder was to be observed by all Israelites

51

in remembrance of God's deliverance from Egyptian bondage and their elevation from slaves of Pharaoh to a holy nation of God's people. The father at the table, presiding as priest, would explain the significance of each item on the table and each action in the observance, lest the glorious story of deliverance be forgotten by the older-ones or never learned by the younger-ones. The salt water on the table, into which the greenery was dipped recalled the tears of those sad years before deliverance. The bitter herbs, not at all enjoyable to the taste-buds, brought to mind the bitterness of life before Jehovah's kind intervention. The lamb, roasted whole, kept the story before the diners that the blood of the lamb, applied to door-posts and lintel, protected the tiny Jewish boys from the plague of death, as the death-angel passed over the homes where the blood was applied. Unleavened bread, rather than the usual leavened bread, recalled with what haste the Jews had to flee across the Red Sea the night of their divine deliverance. Chasoreth, the red sauce on the table, was to keep the people from forgetting the bricks the slaves of Pharaoh were forced to make without the straw that would help hold them together.

Across the centuries this special meal taught lessons of God's past deliverance for Israel. It also was predicting a future rescue from Satan and sin that would far exceed that from Pharaoh and Egypt. The followers of Jesus saw their Master as "the Lamb of God, who takes away the sin of the world" (John 1:29). Paul taught, "Christ, our Passover lamb, has been sacrificed" (I Cor. 5:7). To Christians the unleavened bread spoke of the sinless life of Jesus, untainted by the leaven of iniquity. Today's "Jews for Jesus" call on us to notice the matzos (the corrugated bread used at Passover) are both striped and pierced, foretelling how Christ's hands, feet and side would be pierced and how by his stripes we would be healed. The Christian Jews want us to watch as the father at the table takes the middle of three pieces of bread, breaks it in two, hides it under a pillow and, later, at the drinking of the third cup, retrives the hidden bread before the seder can be ended. The meaning, unknown to non-believing Jews, appears crystal clear to those who have accepted Jesus as God's Messiah. To them the traditional three pieces of bread, separated by linen cloths, represent the Father, the Son and the Holy Spirit. For this reason Jesus took the center matzo and said, "This is my body given for you" (Luke 22:19). The third cup of the Passover meal typified the resurrection of Jesus on the third day.

Whatever the full meaning of each item or action of the last supper of our Lord, as he ate the final Passover with his disciples, it is vital that we get the lesson he intended for the Christian "Lord's Supper" (I Cor. 11:20).

WHAT IS REMEMBERED

From the day the church was born to this present hour every member of the church — the new Israel — has come to a table to "proclaim the Lord's death until he comes" (I Cor. 11:26). Like a magnet, that gospel of Jesus' death, resurrection and return draws all the body of believers together. Christ's prophecy has come to pass. He had spoken, "But I, when I am lifted up from the earth, will draw all men to myself" (John 12:32). The story of the cross has drawn converts to the Savior and the remembrance of that sacrifice of divine love has pulled those converts closer to one another every time they "eat this bread and drink this cup." As different as their cultures or skin-colors, believers from India to Europe or Africa to China, trust in the common gospel and call Jesus their common Lord.

Any coming together requires an agreed time and place. Until the eternal world believers will have jobs to do and children to rear. Being together in assembly every hour of every day cannot be done. When and where to gather are questions requiring an answer. The answer is found on the pages of both New Testament records and early church history. That answer quite surprisingly was neither the 14th to the 21st of Nisan (the Jewish

Passover dates) nor the weekly Sabbath (the Jewish 7th day). The place of assembly became the Lord's Table and the time of assembly became the Lord's Day. The Lord's Supper (χυριαχὸν δεῖπνον) and the Lord's Day (χυριαχὴ ἡμέρα) are found to be joined together. The adjective "Lord's" is used only twice in all the New Testament and they are Revelation 1:10 (Lord's day) and in I Corinthians 11:20 (Lord's supper). This wedding of time and place is a happy marriage. For Sunday was the memorial of Christ's resurrection and the supper was the memorial of Jesus' death. When the setting of the day is linked to the gem of the supper you have the proclamation of the one saving "gospel . . . Christ died for our sins according to the Scriptures . . . (and) he was raised on the third day according to the Scriptures" (I Cor. 15:2-4). Luke described early Christian worship as "the apostles' teaching . . . the fellowship . . . the breaking of bread and . . . prayer" (Acts 2:42) and he recorded how it was "on the first day of the week" that Paul, Silas, the believers in Troas and he "came together to break bread" (Acts 20:7). In the writings of the early church fathers from Justin Martyr and the Didache onward, the meeting time is clearly Sunday, the Lord's Day and the meeting purpose is always the communion or eucharist.

The gospel of Christ and the Christ of the gospel have been and will continue to be the sun around which the different planets and stars will orbit. In him is our unity. Each observance of the Supper from the frozen North to way below the Equator is a testimony to the one gospel. Each believer that shares in the bread and drinks of the cup is testifying that the body and blood of Christ is the source of his or her life. All the family at the table of God is, by the backward glance, remembering that God loves each of us and wants to help us. The upward look reminds that he lives and is able to help us. The inward focus, as the worshiper "examine(s) himself," is to discover the point of his present need (cp. I Cor. 11:28). The hopeful forward glimpse "until he comes" (11:26) anticipates eternity. The words, "I will come back and take you to be with me" (John 14:3), were spoken at the institution of the communion meal.

The next time you sit at the Lord's Table measure its dimensions. You will discover at a moment's Biblical reflection that this table is so high it reaches heaven, yet so low the humblest child of God can sit there. The table is so long it reaches from an upper-room in Jerusalem (possibly the home of John Mark's mother) to the end of history. And it is so broad that there is room for every one of God's family — "red and yellow, black and white" — rich or poor, correct or incorrect, etc. Let's turn to that topic of openness now.

WHO CAN PARTAKE?

As surely as passover was a feast for all Israel, the communion is a feast for all disciples of Christ. With the original disciples, Jesus "took the cup, gave thanks and offered it to them, saying, "Drink from it, all of you" (Matt. 26:27). The KJV "drink ye all of it" might lead a reader to think that the meaning is to empty the cup until all of its contents are gone. Now there is a sense in which the worshiper ought to drink all of the forgiveness, all the blessings and all the memories that are there. But literally the invitation was that all present were welcome to drink from the cup. No believers were excluded. From the beginning, the supper was an affirmation of the unity of all believers in the one family of God.

When you are old enough to have a grown family, you know the heart-break of a father having set a Thanksgiving table for all of his children and then some are unable to come to the family feast. One son or daughter, not at his or her place at the table, and an inner sadness takes away the intended perfect joy. In a small way we can sense how the heavenly Father feels when some of His own "give up meeting together" (Heb. 10:25). The table-fellowships were "love feasts" (Jude 12, cp. II Pet. 2:13) to which Jesus invited his people. Early Christians pointed to Jesus as the Host who had established the table, specified the food for that table and had issued the invitation. They had never considered him the victim *hostia*, as at Roman altars, in what they call the daily sacrifice of the mass. The apostolic church knew Christ to be not the host on the table but our Host at his table. In apostolic times the table had not been changed to an altar, high and lifted up.

Alexander Campbell considered it fitting for an assembly building to have the table in the center of the room with the family seated around it. Perhaps you have been to a theater-in-the-round where the play goes on in the center of the audience which is seated around about. In that kind of a setting one feels a part of the action. In a Gothic structure one is apt to see at the far end an elevated altar and in between the backs of many undistinguishable heads betwixt that table and himself. To Campbell it was important for a gathered congregation to feel invited to share in the supper. He could not forget how as a former Seceder Presbyterian, having passed the test of orthodoxy, he had been given the communion token allowing his access to the table, but lack of that token forbade the right of partaking to others who also called Jesus Lord. Guests at the table of another do not have the right to exclude other guests invited by the Host. The Lord alone has the prerogative to invite. It is a usurpation of Christ's authority to debar any he has invited to his table.

The Biblical, "A man ought to examine himself before he eats of the bread and drinks of the cup" (I Cor. 11:28), is a far cry from you having to pass my criteria for orthodoxy before I allow you to a table that does not belong to me. It is a congregation's privilege to spread the Lord's table. It is the individual's right to examine himself.

The table is for Christians. In New Testament days all of these were immersed believers. Churches committed to restoring the faith and practice of apostolic days baptize all who come to faith. Yet, at the same time of communion, they do not forbid any who count themselves Christians. You often hear it said, "We neither

56

invite nor debar." This terminology stems from the awareness of whose table it is. If visitors are not kept from praying or singing with the gathered flock, they will not be hindered from access to the loaf and cup which is meant for all Christ's people. In the Romanism of the middle ages, the priest, at the end of his homily and prior to the celebration of communion, would say to the visitor, *"Ite, missa est"* that is, "You are dismissed." This allowed the unbaptized to leave, for the Supper would only have significance to one in covenant with Christ. Just as you wash before you eat, a convert would share in the bath of baptism before dining at the family table.

This idea of an "open communion" or a "free table" is still a hard truth to swallow among many parts of the ecumenical movement to this day. The time has not yet arrived that Catholic or Anglican or Fundamentalist are seen breaking bread together in a communion service. The Catholic's table is still closed. The Anglican's table is still closed. But the Lord's table will ever be open to all followers of that Lord until he decides to close it. "This is my body, which is for you" (I Cor. 11:24), said Jesus. Who dare tell one of his disciples, "It is not for you."

I rejoice to be a part of a congregation that is open in attitude. When there is singing praise to God, everyone is welcome to join in. When it is time to pray, all are invited to bow their hearts in intercession. When the message from God's word is preached, each person is open to receive it. When the invitation hymn is sung, anyone who has neither accepted Jesus before or been baptized is offered the opportunity to obey the gospel. So with communion. The table is spread at Christ's command. His invitation is given. We do not forbid any who consider themselves followers of Christ, not because we lack either the machinery or the nerve to do so, but because we accept the concept that the Lord's Supper is a testimony to the fact that Christ's church is one. As E. Stanley Jones wrote in one of his books, "If Communion leads to communion with Christ and with all others who belong to Christ, then it is the Holy Communion. But if it leads to exclusiveness and special claims about validities, then it is an unholy communion. One greater than the Communion is here."

"For anyone who eats and drinks without recognizing the body of the Lord eats and drinks judgment on himself" (I Cor. 11:29). It gives us concern that such a penalty will fall on those who do not "discern" (KJV) the body. The Greek, διαχρίνω, begins with the preposition διά, meaning through. The latter part of the word means to judge or look. I often have trouble *looking through* a telescope or microscope lens. I find myself looking *at* the glass rather than *through* it to the star above or the specimen between glass that I am to study. We need to look beyond the bread and the fruit of the vine to the historic realities of which they speak. The strength from the Supper is not in the calories on the plate or in the cup. The reforming power is in the remembrance. After remembering Calvary, the empty tomb and our acceptance of that redeeming story, do not stop "recognizing the body." In the context of I Corinthians Christ's "body" often refers to the church. Can the "body of Christ" in I Corinthians 10:16 and 11:27,29 be shorn of its meaning in 12:14,15,16,17,19,20 and 27, where the phrase has reference to the church? Paul even asserts to the Corinthians that although the table at their assembly was spread, "when you come together, it is not the Lord's Supper you eat" (I Cor. 11:20). That was because of their unbrotherly actions and divisions at a table intended to proclaim their unity in Christ.

All of them had shared in the "one baptism" that was tied to their acceptance of the "one faith" (Eph. 4:5, cp. Mark 16:15) in their initial conversion. Now as baptized believers they were sharing in the "one loaf" (I Cor. 10:17). The "one baptism," that dramatized redemption's story was the ceremony initiating Christian fellowship. The "one loaf" was the ritual continuing the fellowship based on the gospel story. To that story "there are three that testify: the Spirit, the water and the blood" (I John 5:7-8). The Spirit's testimony in the word, the water of baptism and the blood of the grape at the table agree to the Gospel tradition of the amazing, inclusive grace of the cross.

There is One baptism, but many rivers and pools of water in which that baptism can be shared; One loaf, but broken so everyone can participate; One cup, but as many containers as geography or hygiene dictate; One church, but tens of thousands of gathering places across the world; One Bible, but as many translations as needed for the world to know of the Savior. You best manifest the oneness of the church when in your meditation you think of Christ, all the members in your local body of believers and all your brothers and sisters across the globe. Some may meet in a glass cathedral, some in a native hut, others in an average home or a "church house" provided with pews. But, "discern" and "recognize" the whole church, and the desired unity will be the closer to reality.

WHO CAN SERVE?

If some ecumenists have their way, only ordained clergy will be permitted to celebrate communion. The laying on of hands by those claiming apostolic succession is considered by them a prerequisite for valid communion. The dilemma, facing the denominations working in the ecumenical movement of our time, is that in spite of all the many international and interdenominational gatherings held to date, there has never been a communion service in which all could join. Anglicans, Romanists and others have their fences.

But there is a better way. There is a Biblical way. The New Testament affirmation of the priesthood of all believers cuts across all denominational clergyism. Across the centuries from Century One, the so called "laity" has considered it within a congregation's right to baptize converts or set the table, even if no territorial "bishop" was present. Every congregation, large or small, could select persons to preside, to pray, to bring lessons from Scripture or to pass the elements to the flock.

The story is told that, when King Arthur ruled Britain, he had a goodly group of kights. In spite of their loyalty to him, some of these knights were jealous of one another. They were found to quarrel with one another over their seating in relation to King Arthur. Who got to sit at the head table was the disagreement that led to bitter feelings and even bloodshed. The wise king's solution was to have a "round table" made for his knights, so that all would be equal. King Jesus had the wisdom to have his table (of whatever shape) to have no seats that only a few could fill. "Clericalism" was out. That made possible congregational gatherings for worship and instruction across the American frontier and throughout small farming communities, where seminary-trained preachers were few and far-between in earlier times. These brethren took the Head of the church seriously when he taught, "Where two or three come together in my name, there am I with them" (Matt. 18:20). In many communities believers met Lord's Day after Lord's Day for the supper of remembrance with an appointed elder seeing that the table was spread. Under such care there would be decency and order, as prayer and praise and Bible study were enjoyed.

Such gatherings reminded them that they were a part of the universal body of Christ. The people felt the truth that they were of a kingdom that had spread throughout the earth. The worshiper was transported in his thoughts to the holy land were Jesus walked. In the reading of Scripture, the voice of their Savior was heard. In the breaking of the bread, their souls were lifted to the presence of God and they found strength for another week of hard labor. In prayer for those present or those absent, they felt God was with them.

History books tell that when Ulysses was on his way home to Ithaca at the end of the Trojan War, he was ready to set sail from the island where he was. His friend Calypso came to the beach from which he would set sail. The parting words of Calypso to Ulysses were, "Say goodby to me, but not to the thought of me." In communion we enjoy the thoughts we have of Christ. But there is more than thoughts of Jesus, there is his presence. And where he is, his followers can obey his words, "Do this in remembrance of me" (I Cor. 11:24). The result of both remembering him and all for whom he died is the sensing of being a part of the one church, Christ's body.

UNITY AND THE PRAYER OF THE SAVIOR

God's desire for the oneness of His people is evident in Bible verses, church pictures and Lord's supper observances, but never more clearly than in Jesus' high-priestly prayer of John 17. All historical unity efforts, including that of the twentieth century's Ecumenical Movement have made that prayer its charter.

Jesus packed his life with prayer from the first to the last. While the New Testament does not propose to give us a detailed biography of our Lord's activities, it does record for us sixteen of his prayers.[1] The prayer on the way to the cross is the one that is the longest and goes the deepest into the subject of our study on unity.

Before we hear that intercession regarding us, let us tiptoe to the place where our Savior is praying. In the quietness notice *who* it is that prays. It is the Son of God, talking with his Father. There is much to be learned regarding prayer by listening to the one who best knows how to communicate with heaven. Pay attention to the fact of *when* the Lord is praying. He has left the upper room and is on his way to Gethsemane, the trial, the cross and the grave. No one on his "death bed" will chatter with anyone about issues that do not matter to him. Only concerns of prime importance are discussed at such a time. Unity of believers is of primary concern to him. Now take notice *how* he prays. It is audible. It did not need to be. Like you, Jesus many times could have communed with his Father heart to heart with but a whisper. Yet, on this occasion, the Master speaks loudly enough for John to hear — John to remember — and John later to record words he wanted the church through the ages to know he prayed for them. They were pleas to God for our harmony.

In this intercessory prayer, Jesus, having prayed for himself (John 17:1-5) and for the disciples who were present with him (17:6-14), then utters the plea to God for all believers to come to oneness (17:20-26). For those with him then, the appeal to God was, "Holy Father, protect them by the power of your name . . . so that they may be one as we are one" (17:11). For us, the Lord added:

> I pray also for those who will believe in me through their message, that all of them may be one, Father, just as you are in me and I am in you. May they also be in us so that the world may believe that you have sent me. I have given them the glory that you gave me, that they may be one as we are one. . . . May they be brought to complete unity to let the world know that you sent me and have loved them even as you have loved me (17:20-23).

The unity Jesus knows we will all enjoy in the future of heavenly bliss, he wants us to experience in the historical present. At the end of the apostolic age, when John writes the prayer he had heard many decades before, he longs for that prayer's fulfillment in his time and place. In that day there were schisms and heresies, as is reflected in the Johanine epistles. These were troubling believers throughout all Asia Minor.

THE PRAYER: ITS FOCUS

It is instructive to ask, "Exactly for whom is Jesus praying, when he asks, 'that all of them' may be one?" Is this a prayer for the union of all religions? Is Christ calling on God to unify Jews, Moslems, Hindus and Buddhists? Does Christ want his followers to attempt with the Bahai to combine, eclectically, some of the good insights from each of the world religions? When Edwin T. Dahlberg was president of the National Council of Churches, he proposed going "even beyond the boundaries of the Christian religion." Whatever view you take toward such an inclusiveness, that suggestion is foreign to Jesus' prayer. His concern in John 17 is for those who come to believe in him through the apostles' testimony.

Is the prayer of the Lord that all church agencies, created to assist the church in its mission, be combined? Is the burden of the prayer that all national Bible societies be unified and that all Christian colleges closed down except one? You rather pick up from Jesus' prayer that the oneness he calls for will be followed by such evangelistic success that more Bibles will need to be printed and more Christian educational institutions will need to be created to train leadership for the growing church.

Listen to the words of the prayer again and listen for any request for a unity by force. Is there any hint that heretics ought to be burned at the stake so the one truth will prevail? Was the sword or the flame to be used on a John Hus or a Dr. Servitus for the sake of unity? You know that the answer has to be both "No" and "Never." You also need to learn that there is a unity of force, even when no death is demanded by those in power. Sincere young preachers can find quite threatening a "bishop's"(?) warning to keep in the party line or they will never find another church of that denomination open to them. Consciences have been seared because economic pressure, when there is a family to feed, can be as effective in quieting a reformer's voice as a weapon of death. Some things are worse than division. A union maintained by the loss of liberty is not the Christian ideal.

If the unity for which Christ prayed is not a unity by force, could it be a unity by the opposite of coercion — indifference? If religionists hold their tenets with little conviction, any compromise for the sake of harmony would be all right with them. A church without backbone, or a church teaching whatever is popular at the moment, is not the church revealed in Scripture.

Jesus' prayer was not even a prayer that twenty-nine or so of the denominations of the 20th Century link up. The "them" in John 17 has not to do with corporations but with Christians. The unity is individual not institutional. Denominational loyalty is not the subject-matter of Christ's prayer. Personal loyalty to his "name" (17:11) and his "truth" or "word" (17:17) is the burden of the intercession of our High Priest. The envisioned unity had nothing to do with meeting in the same building or with each congregation supporting financially the same missionary. What then was it?

THE PRAYER: ITS BURDEN

Christian unity — that for which Jesus prayed four times in this one chapter of John — is based on Christ's atonement and his intention of bringing salvation to the world. It is a unity "that the world may believe" (17:21) and that the world may "know" that God sent Christ and "loved them" (17:23). It is a oneness as exemplified in the relation of the Father with the Son and a oneness maintained by our relationship with both the Father and the Son. The believers' unity is a unity given by God. As Jesus said, "I have given them the glory that you gave me, that they may be one as we are one" (17:22). Only God could so change men that, when they come to Him, they can become concerned like he is for the lost of the world.

Church unity is unity in mission. Jesus and his Father were one in purpose. Earlier in the Gospel of John Jesus brings salva-

66

tion to the woman at the well, calling it his "food . . . to do the will of him who sent (him) and to finish his work" (4:34). He states as his reason for coming incarnate, "I have come down from heaven . . . to do the will of him who sent me" (6:38). He specifies, "My Father's will is that everyone who looks to the Son and believes in him shall have eternal life" (6:40). So, in the prayer of John 17, the Lord, ready to complete his mission by dying for the lost, prays, "I have brought you glory on earth completing the work you gave me to do" (17:4).

No church union with another purpose than world salvation is worthy of the designation Christian unity. As Donald G. Bloesch has written, "The goal of authentic ecumenism is not a super-church with power and prestige but rather a worldwide fellowship of belivers united under the Word and dedicated to the conversion and salvation of mankind."[2] Marcellus J. Kik agrees, "Organizational unity, where the one purpose of proclaiming redemption does not exist, will fail to impress the unbelieving world."[3] This unity in mission must be more than a purely spiritual unity or it will not be visible enough to draw the world's attention to Christ.

THE PRAYER: ITS EXAMPLE

To be a disciple, is to be like the Master. In the face of potential division among his followers, what did he do? And by inference, what does he want his followers to do? Knowing that God alone is able to make and keep us one, Jesus went to his Father in prayer. Put it down as an axiom: the most effective single method of coping with disunity is prayer. Prayer is a very small word for a very big thing. Someone has said that there are three stages in doing the work God has assigned. They are "impossible," "difficult" and "done." Observing the divided state of Christendom, one is apt to think "impossible," — when confronting the need for unifying Christian forces. But, reading the

Book that produces faith by its hearing, one must add that while it will be "difficult," through prayer it will be "done." The church can be put on its feet when it is put on its knees.

Prayer is not an easy way to get our wants fulfilled. It is the revealed way to get God's will done on earth as it is in heaven. The Teacher told his followers, "I will do whatever you ask in my name, so that the Son may bring glory to the Father. You may ask me for anything in my name, and I will do it" (John 14:13-14). John R. Rice is convinced that many are forgers in prayer, putting Christ's name to a prayer he would not sign by seeking that which he would not endorse. But to pray in Jesus' name — or according to his will, or for his sake — is never out of order, when we ask for the salvation of men or the oneness of the believers that draws the lost to him. Such a prayer is not, "Thy will be changed," but "Thy will be done."

What can you do for the cause of unity? Jesus went to pray. How about you and me? Should not our tears for the division in Jesus' body, cause us to unite those tears with his? The greatest work on earth is soul-winning and the greatest privilege on earth is to kneel in prayer for a united church, getting up then to help answer that prayer. The old saying that prayer changes things is only overshadowed by the fact that prayer will so change you that God can make you a tool to accomplish His purpose.

There are slick, icy roads through snowy mountains that your car may not be able to cross with your smooth tires. Put on the chains and you can make it. All the potential power in the engine and all the gallons of gas in the tank, will not move your car forward in some places without traction devices. On the road to unity the church has often spun its wheels and made little progress. When we unite in prayer — real prayer — we will unite in fact. The promise is, "You will seek me and find me when you seek me with all your heart" (Jer. 29:13). That means unity is within our grasp, when we care enough about our divided condition that we earnestly go to God with our cry. Prayer only reaches the heights when it comes from the depths. Somewhere I read that prayer means everything to God only when it means everything to the man who offers it.

Are we ready to "pray for the peace of Jerusalem," asking "May there be peace within your walls" (Psa. 122:6-7)? Are we serious about following the examples of the apostles when they showed the way of churchly concern? Can you sincerely say to a congregation, "constantly I remember you in my prayers at all times" (Rom. 1:9-10 cp. Phile. 4)? Are these words your words to your church, "I have not stopped giving thanks for you, remembering you in my prayers. I keep asking that . . . you may know him better" (Eph. 1:16-17 cp. Col. 1:9)? Do you "devote yourself to prayer" (Col. 4:2) with such energy that you can be said to be "always wrestling in prayer" (Col. 4:12)? For the sake of promoting the oneness for which Jesus prayed, let us "pray continually" (I Thess. 5:17) for the whole church's wholeness. What good will that do? Paul told the church of his time, "You help us by your prayers" (1:11). James asked that we "pray for each other . . . (for) the prayer of a righteous man is powerful and effective" (James 5:16). Whatever else we can or will do, "first of all," there are prayers (and) intercessions," otherwise there can not be "peaceful and quiet lives" (I Tim. 2:1-2).

If you believe the Book and want the oneness, you start with prayer. E. M. Bounds made the observation:

> What the church needs today is not more machinery or better, not new organizations or more and novel methods, but men whom the Holy Ghost can use — men of prayer, men mighty in prayer. The Holy Ghost does not flow through methods, but through men. He does not come on machinery, but on men. He does not anoint plans, but men — men of prayer.

One thing we know, disciples may fall asleep when Jesus prays, but he will never sleep while any of us seek his face.

You can't keep praying for unity without beginning to really desire it. Decide if you really want harmony in your congregation and with all the others with whom you have contact. If you are serious, the dangerous thing is that your prayer will be answered, possibly bringing more than you intended. A prayer for strength may bring obstacles with which you must struggle to develop that strength. In the same way an asking for the Spirit of Christ within so that you might contribute to the unity solution, might cause your eyes to open wider than ever before. You could begin to see good in other believers you had failed to recognize before. Your arms might lengthen to reach out toward others you prior to this did not desire to fellowship. The old sectarian garb that used to feel so comfortable on you might have become too restrictive and narrow for your expanding mind and heart.

Jesus prayed. I should pray. We should pray together. The focus should be those who believe in Christ. The burden should be ONE CHURCH, so that there may be a WON WORLD. The example should be that when you and I pray as Christ prayed, each petitioner adds to the oratorio of prayer until the crescendo of perfect unity is reached.

Carlton C. Buck, the author of the hymn "I Believe in Miracles," has more recently given us "When The Savior's Prayer Is Answered." It goes:

> When the Savior's prayer is answered,
> Whether here or over there
> And at last the total victory is won;
> Then the saints will be triumphant
> With the joy of answered prayer
> Singing Glory hallelujah to the Son
>
> When the true Church is together
> In the final victory
> What a hymn of joyous triumph it will raise;
> When the Savior's prayer is answered,
> What rejoicing there will be,
> All together, one in Christ, to sing His praise.

We can help to bring the answer
To the Savior's fervent prayer
By submitting to His good and perfect will;
We, the Church, can learn to follow,
And His longing, we can share,
For in Heaven He is interceding still.

Jesus loved the Church He founded.
Knew that Satan would assail,
And He prayed that all believers might be one;
Though He knew there would be hardship,
Yet the Church would still prevail
Finding oneness like the Father and the Son.[4]

Endnotes

1. Matthew 11:25-27; 19:13; 26:36; Mark 1:35; 6:46; Luke 3:21-22; 5:16; 6:12; 9:18-21,28; 11:1; 22:32; 23:46; John 11:41-42; 12:27-28; 17:1-26.
2. *The Reform of the Church,* (Grand Rapids: Eerdmans, 1970), p. 184.
3. *Ecumenism and the Evangelical,* (Philadelphia: The Presbyterian and Reformed Publishing Co., 1958).
4. Copyright 1988 by Carlton C. Buck & Lawrence Crook. Used by permission (For complete song, P.O. Box 211, Eugene, OR 97440).

5

UNITY AND THE PERSONS OF THE GODHEAD

Thousands of times in the Bible we meet the word "God" or "Lord." In only one Bible book (Esther) God is not mentioned by name. In only one New Testament chapter (I Cor. 13) is His name missing. The Creator-Redeemer is the leading character in the book of Scripture and the primary advocate of church unity.

If polytheism were a reality, one would expect thousands of gods to equal multitudes of religions. But from Genesis to Revelation the Scripture affirms monotheism to be the truth. The fatal flaw in denominationalism is that it seems to deny before the world God's unity, as surely as polytheism does. Polydenominationalism is as Biblically contradictory as polytheism. The unity of Christians would more properly reflect the unity of God. Theodore O. Wedel, in the Epistle to the Ephesians' portion of *The Interpreter's Bible*, writes:

This monotheism of the Bible stands in judgment over disunited

73

Christianity today. Are we worshipping one God, or are we worshipping a multitude of Baals?[1]

GOD IS ONE

The Christian affirms, "There is . . . one God and Father of all, who is over all and through all and in all" (Eph. 4:4-6). Hinduism today speaks of more than 333,000,000 deities. Pliny reports that the Athens of Nero's day had 3,000 public statues of gods, to say nothing of the private houses with their protecting gods beyond number. In that very time Paul affirmed:

> We know that an idol is nothing at all in the world and that there is no God but one. For even if there are so-called gods . . . yet for us there is but one God (I Cor. 8:4-6).

To this agreed the tables of stone with the inscription, "You shall have no other gods before me" (Exod. 20:3, Deut. 5:7). To this corresponded the words of the prophets:

> Since ancient times no one has heard, no ear has perceived, no eye has seen any God besides you, who acts on behalf of those who wait for him (Isa. 64:4).

To this harmonized the *shema*, "The LORD our God, the LORD is one" (Deut. 6:4).

It is sometimes claimed that monotheism is not in all the Old Testament for the Hebrew word for God is a plural noun. *Elohim* is a plural noun but in every case of its usage the verb that follows is singular (cp. Gen. 1:1,26; 3:22; 11:7; Isa. 6:8). Grammarians call *Elohim* either the plural of majesty or a plural because it is denoting the sum of all God's powers and attributes. Still others find the hint of the Trinity in unity.

To affirm the oneness of God is to recognize Him as the origin and goal of the universe, the One who reigns over the past, the

74

present and the future, the One altogether unique. "The LORD is God and there is no other" (I Kings 8:60). The name of the prophet Micah means, "Who is like Jehovah?" That is the question raised by the song of Moses and Miriam after the exodus crossing of the Red Sea, "Who among the gods is like you, O LORD? Who is like you — majestic in holiness, awesome in glory, working wonders?" (Exod. 15:11).

Pagan gods are multiple because they are finite. The Christian God is one, for he is absolute. He fills all space (I Kings 8:27), has all wisdom (Job 12:12), is not limited to time (Psa. 90:2) and lacks no power (Luke 1:37). Reason, nature and revelation join in the doxology, "Now to the King eternal, immortal, invisible, the only God, be honor and glory for ever and ever. Amen." (I Tim. 1:17). Believers from East and West look forward to the promised day when "there will be one LORD, and his name the only name" (Zech. 4:9).

The point being made in the Bible's declaration that God is one[2], is that monotheism stands in judgment over His worshiper's disunity. The questions to be answered are, "Have we not all one Father? Did not one God create us? Why do we profane the covenant . . . by breaking faith with one another?" (Mal. 2:10). "Is God the God of Jews only? Is he not the God of Gentiles too? . . . there is only one God" (Rom. 3:29-30). Could it be that we are not one with our brothers beside us for our perfect harmony with the God above us has been broken? In the early pages of Genesis it was the rupture of fellowship with God that led to the loss of unity amongst men. At the least we ought to recognize that the ultimate foundation of the unity we seek is God himself. Our close unity with him will be reflected in our unity with those who belong to him.

GOD IS LOVE AND LIGHT

"Anyone who comes to (God) must believe that he exists"

(Heb. 11:6) and, everyone who has come to him, has learned that "God is love" (I John 4:8,16) and "God is light" (I John 1:5). This character affirmation regarding God speaks to the nature of the unity he wants for his people. A unity of love and compassion, of mercy and grace, of benevolence and goodness was suggested by Jesus' prayer that the believers be one as he and the Father were one (John 17:22). The world's people needed to learn that the relationship between the Father and the Son was one of love and that that love included them. "The Father of Compassion" (II Cor. 1:3) begets children of compassion.

It is impossible to overemphasize that any unity on earth, with similarities to the unity of heaven's Father and Son, must be a manifestation of love. Someone said, "God's love has a height without a top, a depth without a bottom, a length without an end and a breadth without a limit." A God of love can require no less than love on our part. Love finds its basis in the nature of God. It is not an exterior virtue forced on him from another source. When one is born of God, love of the brotherhood comes naturally for "we are God's workmanship" (Eph. 2:10). John wrote, "Dear friends . . . love comes from God. Everyone who loves has been born of God" (I John 4:7) and "since God so loved us, we also ought to love one another" (4:11). The aged apostle of love had learned by both revelation and experience that, "If anyone says, 'I love God,' yet hates his brother, he is a liar . . . Whoever loves God must also love his brother" (4:20-21). Not to love is to be ungodly and "anyone born of God does not continue to sin" (5:18). To be unbrotherly is to sin. To walk in love is to follow the path of peace and not the road of division that leads to destruction.

The apostle to the Gentiles pronounced peace upon the churches and understood that God is the source of all harmony, as Satan is the originator of strife. Paul's letters are apt to begin, "Peace to you from God our Father" (Eph. 1:2, cp. Phil. 1:2; Col. 1:2; II Thess. 1:2; I Tim. 1:2; II Tim. 1:2; Titus 1:4) or to conclude, "Peace to the brothers, and love with faith from God the Father" (Eph. 6:23). Paul knew God to be "the God of peace" (I Thess. 5:23; Rom. 15:33, cp. Heb. 13:20). A fighting, fussing, haranguing congregation may call itself a church of God, but it is more likely a case of false advertising. Where Jesus is Lord, the "Lord of peace himself (is known to) give . . . peace at all times and in every way" (II Thess. 3:16). Where men are being reborn, they are "to be made new in the attitude of (their) minds" (Eph. 4:23). They are expected to "be imitators of God . . . as dearly loved children and (to) live a life of love" (Eph. 5:1-2). He who is divisive serves another king than the "king of peace" (Heb. 7:2).

While the nature of God as love speaks to the kind of unity we are to look for, so does his quality of light. "In him there is no darkness at all" (I John 1:5). No blot of untruth is to be made a permanent part of tomorrow's uniting efforts. The unchanging God ill befits a constantly changing theology. The oneness of the Father and Son, stressed in Christ's prayer for unity, includes harmony in love, in purpose and also in doctrine. Can you even imagine a situation where Jesus would say, "The Father holds this view, but I totally disagree?" He rather was always declaring, "My teaching is not my own. It comes from him who sent me" (John 7:16), or "He who sent me is reliable, and what I have heard from him I tell the world . . . I do nothing on my own but speak just what the Father has taught me" (John 8:26,28, cp. 12:49-50).

GOD IS TRIUNE

The doxology our congregations sing may hint to us that the unity we seek and the unity of heaven is inter-personal. Christians lift up their voices, "Holy, holy, holy, Lord God Almighty . . . God in three persons, blessed Trinity." I am quick to admit that the word trinity is not a Biblical term and that Tertullian (A.D. 160-240) was the first to use it. I am also more than ready to concede my difficulty in adequately explaining "the arithmetic of heaven" to an inquirer's satisfaction. Yes, I can point to a single triangle of three equal sides and label the sides Father, Son and Spirit or I can pick one clover and note three leaves, but the questioner is still confused. I can show that I am a son, a husband and a father at the same time. Or I can tell of an Indian in the frozen North sweeping aside the snow, cutting a hole in the ice that covers the lake and fishing in the water, explaining that snow is water, ice is water and water is water. If that helps, good. But it may not explain the relationship the Bible describes of the Father, the Son and the Holy Spirit. "Beyond all question, the mystery of godliness is great" (I Tim. 3:16). I am not a rationalist ready to repudiate everything I cannot understand. I am a believer that the intention of the Father for man's salvation brought the invasion of the Son into history and now the indwelling of the Spirit is completing our redemption.

The same Bible that asserts God is one, equally affirms the distinction of "the Father and of the Son and of the Holy Spirit" (Matt. 28:20). At Jesus' baptism the Father's voice speaks from heaven, "This is my Son" and "the Spirit of God" descends upon Jesus like a dove (Matt. 3:16-17). A father can not be his own son, nor can a son be his own father. The benediction that closes II Corinthians speaks of "the grace of the Lord Jesus Christ, and the love of God, and the fellowship of the Holy Spirit" (13:14). The pillars of unity include "one Spirit . . . one Lord . . . one God and Father" (Eph. 4:4-6).

Peter knew that our election was based on the "foreknowledge of God the Father . . . the sanctifying work of the Spirit, for obedience to Jesus Christ" (I Pet. 1:2). This revealed mystery that the one true God is manifest in three persons is taken by faith. The finite mind of man can not grasp infinity anymore than a thimble can contain the water of the seven seas.

Divine revelation speaks of "God, the Father" (I Cor. 8:6) and also terms Jesus "the Word was God" (John 1:1). In Acts we learn that to "have lied to the Holy Spirit" is to "have lied . . . to

God" (5:3-4). The attributes of deity assigned to one is attributed to the others. Each person is said to be eternal (Rom. 16:26; Rev. 22:13; Heb. 9:14); holy (Rev. 4:8; 15:4; Acts 3:14; I John 2:20); omnipresent (Jer. 23:24; Eph. 1:23; Psa. 139:7); omnipotent (Gen. 17:1; Rev. 1:8; Rom. 15:9; Jer. 32:17; Heb. 1:3; Luke 1:35); omniscient (Acts 15:8; John 21:17; I Cor. 2:9-11); creator (Gen. 1:1; Col. 1:16; Job 33:4; Psa. 148:5; John 1:3), *et al.*

For our purposes realize that the church enjoys fellowship with an undenominational Father, an undenominational Savior, an undenominational Spirit. It does not point us to a man-made idol, carved to my specification and used to back my ideas. You and I belong to him who stands ready to transform us. We ought not look at him as ours to be used at our will and whim. Our relationship to one another in the church is to be as close, vital and real as that between the Father, Son and Spirit. The church is to mirror the tri-unity of God. There is communication amongst the members of the "godhead" (KJV, Acts 17:29; Rom. 1:20; Col. 2:9). The unicity of deity is as personal as the oneness sought by his human family. Jesus, who said, "I and the Father are one" (John 10:30) and "Anyone who has seen me has seen the Father" (John 14:9), called on the Father to make us who believe on him to be as one as they (John 17:20-21).

A look at the God of the Bible is to see but one God and therefore one Church. To find his character as love and light is to discover that the unity of his followers is to be both a fellowship in love and in the light of truth he has revealed. To uncover the mystery of one God in three persons is to discover that unity with God and his worshipers is much more inter-personal than it is mechanical. The unity from heaven is a gift from God to his people, not a human effort to organize, theorize and unionize the religious sects that have sprung up over the years.

ONE FATHER, ONE FAMILY

Endnotes

1. Volume 10 (New York: Abingdon Press, 1953), p. 687.
2. Cp. Deuteronomy 4:35; Isaiah 43:10; 44:6; 45:5,14,18,22; 46:9; Matthew 4:10; Luke 4:8; John 17:3; Galatians 3:20; I Timothy 2:5; 6:15; Hebrews 6:13; James 2:19; 4:12; Jude 25.

6

UNITY AND THE PURPOSE OF THE CHURCH

The camp song goes on and on: "We're here, because we're here, because we're here, because we're here." This ditty does not pass for a church hymn because it does not explain why the church is here. Without a clear purpose — without a sense of mission — without a realization of why the church is in the world, we fail to grasp why unity of the body of believers has such a priority to God.

Did you ever wonder why a convert "buried" and "raised" in the waters of baptism (Rom. 6:4), did not immediately ascend to heaven, the final destination of the redeemed? Why did God will that those with "citizenship . . . in heaven" (Phil. 3:20) stick around on earth? The Bible answer is: "Make disciples of all nations" (Matt. 28:19), "preach the good news" (Mark 16:15) of "repentance and forgiveness of sins" (Luke 24:47). We baptized-believers should join Paul in accepting our divine task, affirming, "We proclaim him (Christ), admonishing and teaching everyone . . . so that we may present everyone perfect in Christ. To this end I labor" (Col. 1:28-29).

Once we understand that evangelism is the church's business, we immediately grasp why division is such an onus and unity is such a need. We see why Jesus tied the salvation of the lost to the harmony of the saved, when he prayed "that all of them may be one . . . that the world may believe" (John 17:20-21).

THE WHY OF ONENESS

A slogan of the Restoration Movement that heralded, "We have no book but the Bible, no creed but the Christ and no name but the Divine" needs to add, "No goal but to save." It ought to be apparent that we can not multiply at the same time we divide. It is informative to learn that the present ecumenical movement of today grew out of the modern missionary movement's awareness that denominationalism was blunting its witness. A disunited church has its counterpart in a disbelieving world. It seemed evident that the order was not going to be, win the world first and then get together for a big celebration; but be one so the church will have a chance of winning that religiously confused world.

Myron J. Taylor, in a sermon to the Westwood Hills Christian Church of Los Angeles, said,

> The greatest hindrance to the Gospel today is the division in the church. Many sincere people who would like to be related to God in their lives are befuddled and confused by the babble of confusing sectarian tongues. The world can never be led to faith in Christ until first the Church demonstrates its loyalty to Him. Christian unity is required by God's design for the Church, by the will of Christ, by the very concept of a Church, by the work the Church has to do.

If missions abroad and soul-winning at home is to be the task to which we pledge, "This 'one thing I do' " (Phil. 3:13), then the enabling factor of unity demands attention. Jesus who "came to seek and to save what was lost" (Luke 19:10), is the one who prayed for unity. Barton W. Stone, the intensely evangelistic giant among the fathers of the Reformation of the 19th Century, is the one who challenged, "let unity be our polar star." The salvation of mankind and the unity of believers have been joined together and ought not be separated. The goal is redemption, the means to that end is the church "being one in spirit and purpose" (Phil. 2:2). The world is too strong to be conquered by a divided church.

In a disciplined army, men move as a body under the direction of one mind. In an undisciplined mob each individual follows his own influences. Let it be "God who works in you to will and to act according to his good purpose" (Phil. 2:13). His good purpose is that the world know of his Son to their reconciliation.

THE WAY TO ONENESS

The why of oneness is the world's salvation. But, what is the way to that oneness? At a North American Christian Convention several years ago a speaker (who it was I regret I have forgotten) told of a Methodist Bishop commenting on a proposed merger of the Methodist Church in England with the Anglican Church. His query was, "I have always wondered what the union of two corpses would produce." It is not to be negative that I raise the question, "What denominational merger, in the century now passing, has resulted in an upsurge in evangelistic thrust?" Has every-member consciousness to world-mission been the fruit? Or has the sometimes heard accusation found some justification that the least missionary-minded bodies are those with targeted ecumenical concern, while some who seldom use the word ecumenical in their self-description are way ahead in missionary activity.

Please excuse a rather long quote from my former professor,

ONE FATHER, ONE FAMILY

the late Stephen J. England of Phillips University. I cite him because he would be recognized by all as an ecumenist through his associations and his writings. He penned:

> I admit that I have been more than a little disturbed by the apparent correlation between interest in the Ecumenical Movement and the decline in evangelistic effectiveness; and by the other correlation, that between opposition to the Ecumenical Movement and phenomenal growth. It is a fact, however one may explain it, that those Christian groups which most decisively have nothing to do with union negotiations are exactly those which are growing most rapidly. I have no ready explanation of this perverse phenomenon. Perhaps it is due to a one-sided emphasis on Christian union. As various groups admit that it really makes little difference whether one joins this church or that, the man-in-the-street, that legendary and practical fellow, may conclude that it makes no difference whether he joins any of them. A union of denominations, accomplished either by the 'what will you give up' scheme, or by its evil kinsman described at Lund as 'the clever piecing together of our ancestral inheritances,' may produce a hybrid so theologically anemic that it has no message, no evangelistic appeal and no spiritual power. Let us never forget that the first duty of any church is not to unite, but to evangelize; and if it neglects its first duty, it forfeits its God-given reason for existence![1]

The church must never forget that it is God's instrument in restoring humanity to himself. Our *raison detre*, the purpose for our being, is the redemption of the lost for which Jesus died. Reconciliation of men to God is the work of the church. Unity must be welded to evangelistic purpose or it is too limited. Evangelism ought to be synthesized with unity so that it will not fail.

The one heart and soul of the infant church was at its best when they were involved "day after day, in the temple courts and from house to house . . . teaching and proclaiming the good news that Jesus is the Christ" (Acts 5:42). It is well to recall that "Jesus Christ is the same yesterday and today and forever" (Heb.

84

13:8) and, being unchanging, he might still bless us with unity at the point of all of us getting together in the spreading of the story of Jesus and his love.

Merging morgues will not bring revival, but joining hands in lifting souls from the sinking sands of sin will bring renewal everywhere. The why of unity is evangelism. So is the way of unity. Getting back to our single purpose will bring us together. We may have wandered far from home and gone to distant lands of political clout or existential experiences, but every mile back to the great commission will be getting us closer together step by step.

We have looked at Christian unity from six vantage points and found that from every angle our oneness is the Lord's divine will. That is the plain teaching of Scripture. That is the message of each New Testament picture of the church. That is the lesson proclaimed every week at the Lord's Table. That is the burden of Jesus' prayer on the way to his cross. That is the conclusion to which one is driven, who meditates on God and his nature. That is realization of the church in its obedience to its divine assignment. God has willed our oneness. Only Satan could want us splitting into factions and subdivisions. To be aware of the devices of our enemy — "that ancient serpent called the devil, or Satan, who leads the whole world astray" (Rev. 12:9) — is our next study. To recognize the dividing walls he erects to keep us apart, will prepare us to avoid the trap. That is our next adventure.

Endnotes

1. "Union and Unity in the Future: Shadows of Things to Come (II)," (The Christian-Evangelist, December 5, 1956), p. 9.

THE DEVIL'S DIVIDING
WALLS FOR OUR SEPARATIONS

7

UNITY AND THE PROBLEM OF SCHISMS

How can anyone be an Atheist? That question my mind asks as I stroll through the woods or view a bed of flowers. It would be impossible for me to view this awe-inspiring universe and not begin to sing, "The heavens declare the glory of God" (Psa. 19:1). My heart agrees with the Psalmist, "The fool says in his heart, 'There is no God' " (Psa. 14:1). But another problem I have is to hear a theologian deny the reality of Satan in the face of gang shootings, drug inundation and pornographic acceptance. One very convincing evidence of the devil's existence is the schism in the ranks of the church. Peter was right, "Your enemy the devil prowls around like a roaring lion looking for someone to devour" (I Pet. 5:8).

In the New Testament all sin is condemned, but the evil most frequently denounced and most severely condemned is the sin of schism. Classified with "sexual immorality, impurity and debauchery; idolatry and witchcraft" is "discord . . . dissensions, factions" (Gal. 5:19-20). Jude warns of "men who divide you, who follow mere natural instincts and do not have the Spirit" (Jude 19). Even the pagan Roman soldiers who crucified Jesus seeing the value of Christ's undergarment that was "seamless, woven in one piece from top to bottom," said, "Let's not tear it" (John 19:23-24). Don't we wish that the Lord's followers would see the priceless value of his united church and vow never to rend it? The wise Solomon knew he could count on a mother's love to reveal who the true mother was, when two women claimed the baby was hers. Ordering the child to be divided, so each woman could have half, the "woman whose son was alive was filled with compassion for her son and said to the king, 'Please, my lord, give her the living baby!' " (I Kings 3:25-26). True Christians, who love the church, will do anything to avoid schism in the body of believers.

Jesus, growing up in a large family, likely saw his brothers and sisters wear hand-me-down-garments and probably observed his mother patch torn clothes. He noted that "No one sews a patch of unshrunk cloth on an old garment, for the patch will pull away from the garment, making the tear worse" (Matt. 9:16; Mark 2:21). Torn clothes to a mother, rent nets to a fisherman or split congregations to a believer are concerns of top priority. John Calvin in a letter to Cranmer in 1552 revealed how deeply he was worried at the division he saw. He wrote, "Among the greatest evils of our time must be counted the fact that the churches are so disunited. So far as I am concerned, if I can do anything to help, I shall not hesitate to cross ten oceans to serve this cause."

A characteristic of heresy is schism. It separates from the existing religious community because of a particular slant on the teaching. The break-away results in both impoverishment of the members and deformity in the doctrine.

THE PERIL OF SCHISM

The problem of disunity must be seen as the problem of evil, for that is what it is. Division is not to be winked at nor classified as "not so bad." It is costly. It is wasteful. It is a road-block to evangelism. It is an embarrassment to the cause. In the words of Thomas Campbell it is "anti-christian, anti-scriptural, anti-natural."

This evil was warned against by Jesus (Matt. 12:25) and opposed by his disciples (Acts 20:30). To the apostles the greatest heresy of all was breaking fellowship. Paul put up the red-flag against any who have "an unhealthy interest in controversies and quarrels about words that result in envy, strife, malicious talk, evil suspicions and constant friction between men of corrupt mind" (I Tim. 6:4-5). While it is true that we are warned to "not give up meeting together" (Heb. 10:25), it is also a fact that some "meetings do more harm than good" (I Cor. 11:17). What kind of a service could that be? Paul is specific in his answer, "In the first place, I hear that when you come together as a church, there are divisions among you" (11:18).

We must cease to regard division in the family of God as a tool of acceptance for maintaining purity of doctrine, when it may in fact be the devil's ploy to destroy Christ's church. As someone put it, "The devil would rather start a church fuss any time than to sell a case of whiskey." Many times, if not most of the time, a church split is not a matter of orthodoxy versus heterodoxy.

The Irish parliamentarian, T.P. O'Connor, drew on a table cloth a map of Ireland to explain to his friend the discord at home. He went on, "You see the Catholics live down here, while up here dwell the Protestants; and they're at each others throats all the time . . . I often wish they were all heathens so they could live together like Christians." The very word "religion" is from the Latin *religare,* which means to bind back. True religion binds men back to God and to one another. Division into mutually exclusive groups is a denial of the Christian religion. I have heard Protestant Denominationalism termed "a menagerie of quarreling sects." This disgrace is "like gangrene" (II Tim. 2:17) and is "the trap of the devil" (II Tim. 2:26).

W. Carl Ketcherside wrote:

> Life can be sustained only by unity. Death results from disunity.
> This is true in the vegetable, animal and spiritual worlds, those
> three areas in which we are acquainted with life. If a plant or tree
> is dismembered and the process of division continues long
> enough the plant will be killed. If an animal continues to be
> fragmented by removal of limbs and organs, death will result. If
> we bite and devour one another we will be consumed one of
> another.[1]

May the conversation recorded in Zechariah never be repeated in
our time. He wrote, "If someone asks him, 'What are these
wounds on your body?' he will answer, 'The wounds I was given
at the house of my friends,' " (13:6). Friends or brothers are to
act in character.

THE PROGNOSIS OF SCHISM

If the disease of schism, uncured, is fatal, it needs diagnosis,
prognosis and prescription for cure. To find the causes of disunity
is to discover the way to overcome them. Remove the causes and
the cure is on its way. The Devil is a good mathematician
multiplying our problems, dividing our churches and subtracting
our power. He is the author of our indifference and denominational differences. Christ, our Great Physician, is ready to help us
discover our problem and available to bring us the healing we
need.

The word "sin" has an "I" at its center and may suggest that all
sin is self centered. "My will be done" is the cry of the old-nature.
"Thy will be done" is the prayer of those born-again. If your congregation has a "Diotrephes, who loves to be first" (III John 9),
trouble will be coming. Paul foresaw it, when he told the Ephesian elders, "Even from your own number men will arise and
distort the truth in order to draw away disciples after them" (Acts
20:30). That drawing away disciples is how sects always rise. A

personally ambitious religionist gets a new theory and is driven to start a group that will promote his ideas. Such a teacher will "despise authority" (II Pet. 2:10) over him, but become the only authority to all who will subject themselves to his leadership.

Personal ambition is one cause of division and personal favoritism is another. When "one of you says, 'I follow Paul'; another, 'I follow Apollos'; another, 'I follow Cephas' " (I Cor. 1:12), rivalry results. The apostolic warning is not to let "Satan . . . outwit us," but beware "his schemes" (II Cor. 2:11). Satan has found that the ploy of turning Jesus' servants into denominational heads will work most of the time as the distinctive labels "Lutheran, Calvinist, Wesleyan, etc." indicate. When such weeds grow up, it is well to recognize the source of these different seeds. "Where did the weeds come from?" Christ's reply was, "An enemy did this" (Matt. 13:27-28). The gospel of the cross was to unify all men. "Enemies of the cross of Christ" (Phil. 3:18) scatter the flock by their non-apostolic message.

Any diagnosis of our disorder and separation must reveal sectarian teaching as one of our afflictions. That disease of "false doctrine" has been with us from early days and generally does "promote controversies rather than God's work" (I Tim. 1:3-4). Proponents of the novel teaching take believers "captive through hollow and deceptive philosophy, which depends on human tradition and the basic principles of this world rather than on Christ" (Col. 2:8). Who is susceptible? Any who will "gather around them . . . teachers to say what their itching ears want to hear." Such people "turn their ears away from the truth and turn aside to myths" (II Tim. 4:3-4). We all need the Biblical warning, "Do not be carried away by all kinds of strange teachings" (Heb. 13:9). If in ancient days of the church "false brothers had infiltrated our ranks" (Gal. 2:4) and were "zealous to win you over . . . to alienate you from us, so that you may be zealous for them" (Gal. 4:17), the Satanic bait is still being used. To turn to a "different gospel — which is really no gospel at all" (Gal. 1:6-7) is foolishness indeed.

Beware of those "who worm their way into homes" to "oppose the truth" (II Tim. 3:6,8). The "destructive heresies" deny "the sovereign Lord" and "exploit you with stories they have made up" (II Pet. 2:1,3). Paul called them "agitators" (Gal. 5:12). Peter termed them "blots and blemishes" (II Pet. 2:13). John named them "the antichrist" (I John 2:22), because they denied the essential gospel of Christ's incarnation and atonement (II John 7; I John 5:6). One belief is not as good as another. The "apostles' teaching" is the norm by which to distinguish truth from error. The "fellowship . . . with the Father and with his Son, Jesus Christ" remains unbroken when "we walk in the light" (I John 1:3,7). If you would not be "led astray," give no time to someone who "preaches a Jesus other than the Jesus (apostles) preached . . . or a different gospel" (II Cor. 11:3-4). Christ-degrading or gospel-destroying teaching is to be rebuked "sharply" and "no attention" is to be given "those who reject the truth" (Titus 1:13-14). Elders of congregations are to "watch out for those dogs" — the Judaizers — who would scatter the flock (Phil. 3:2). "Stir up trouble" (Phil. 1:17) is the job-description of a schismatic. "Watch out for those who cause divisions" (Rom. 16:17) is an important part of a pastor's job-description.

THE PREVENTION OF SCHISM

A Health Maintenance Organization — an HMO — is built on the assumption that preventative medicine, which stops diseases before they start, is better than allowing a sickness to progress and then trying to overcome it. How can potential schism be eliminated before it weakens Christ's church?

Charles Clayton Morrison many years ago in a Christian Century article challenged the ecumenical leaders of his time, saying, "Any movement for Christian Unity which does not attack the denominational system is destined to be swallowed up by it." If a denomination distinguishes itself from other Christians by its distinctive name or by following a detailed creedal statement or by forming an exclusive governing organization, is there another way?

R.M. Bell, former president of Johnson Bible College, told of two preachers of different denominations in Kentucky a century ago, who decided to conduct a union meeting to win as many converts as possible to Christ. The agreement was that at the end of the soul-winning effort the new converts would be free to choose which of the two denominations to join. It didn't turn out that way. The converts said, "We are already Christians, members of the body of Christ, and we are united, but if some join one denomination and the remaining another, then we would be divided and that is not right." They agreed to continue to meet and worship as the New Testament directed them and to stay one body.

Is that option still available? Can one be a Christian without aligning with a party? Can a congregation just be Christian, no more and no less? To what denomination does obeying the gospel make you belong? While it is easy enough to join a sect of one's choice, there is nothing in the Bible to tell you how to become a denominationalist. The Book only informs on how to become a saved person and how such redeemed people are to serve him.

I belong to no denomination, but am a Christian only, because God wants his children to have the very best. If you are able to see some good in each denomination, the question still comes, Why accept a half-truth or ninety-nine percent of truth? Is that a better choice than all of the truth? When a man links himself to a sect that emphasizes some Biblical truth, but at the same time does not join with a religious body that stresses another Scriptural insight, he has a part when God wished for him the whole. The Bible contains the truth, the whole truth and nothing but the truth. Where a faction may follow a fraction of God's revelation, a congregation is better served being completely, *en toto*, Christian.

R.H. Boll in his tract "Why Not Be Just A Christian?", reasons:

> Every theory, every system, every sect has *some* truth. But *the Christian* has all, has a right to all, and access to all. If any sect in the world holds any portion of truth, the Christian has the greater right to accept and proclaim it. He does not need to join the sect in question to get what truth it may happen to have. He does not even need to sift through the chaff of those human theories. In Christ he has all beforehand.[2]

There were religious parties in the Judaism of Jesus' day. He did not feel it necessary to pledge allegiance to the Pharisee, the Sadducee, the Herodian or the Essene. His commitment to the Heavenly Father made all lesser covenants unnecessary. Why join "the circumcision group" (Titus 1:10) when membership in the church of which the Lord is head is an option?

Let personal ambition give way to humility. Let the refusal to follow men be strengthened by the pledge to follow Christ as Savior and Lord. Let hobby-riding and sectarian teaching fade away in the sunlight of revealed truth. Let the tongue, which can be a sword to cut and sever brother from brother, become a tool of love to bring healing everywhere. "Dear children, keep yourselves from idols" (I John 5:21) and from serving man-made denominations rather than the church Christ created. Some ideas are "falsely called knowledge" (I Tim. 6:20) and some religious institutions are falsely called church.

Zechariah describes a shepherd with two staffs. He writes, "I took two staffs and called one Favor and the other Union, and I pastured the flock." Symbolically he breaks first the staff called Favor and later the one called Union. When God's gracious covenant is broken, the breaking of brotherhood follows. We remain in God's Favor when we reject schism that breaks the bonds of brotherhood.

Endnotes

1. *Deep Roots: Reprint of Mission Messenger 1966*, (Saint Louis, Missouri), p. 67.
2. The Word and Work, Louisville, Kentucky, p. 7.

8

UNITY AND THE PRIDE OF HUMANS

Weddings are happy occasions and the audience rises to its feet when the organ peals out, "Here Comes the Bride." Sadness beclouds the heart, if later, family arguments have led to a separation or a divorce. Then the words of the music may have become, "Here Comes the Pride." Scissors cut cloth and schisms divide churches. In the latter instance Satan's tool in "appealing to the lustful desires of sinful human nature" (II Pet. 2:18) is pride.

We need to be careful here. To see our congregation or religious persuasion as totally orthodox and all others in various degrees of error can lead to a pride — a haughtiness — that may place us under the judgment, "Pride goes before destruction, a haughty spirit before a fall" (Prov. 16:18). I read somewhere, "The biggest impediment to unity is small men. Men who don't marvel at their own redemption aren't big enough to enjoy someone else's."

To have joined a sect to end all sects, or to have created a denomination to end all denominations is not yet to have arrived at non-sectarian, non-denominational Christianity. To develop the attitude that one has attained the ideal — reached the end of the road — could be but the acceptance of a denominational disposition. History records the outcome of many who have set out to heal divisions in the church, but have succeeded only in creating new ones. The goal has been right but the humility has, in some cases, been lacking.

TEST YOUR WORDS

Does an outsider, hearing you state your case, get the impression that you are but a sinner saved by grace? "No one can boast. For we are God's workmanship, created in Christ Jesus" (Eph. 2:9-10). Paul considered himself to have been "the worst of sinners" (I Tim. 1:16). He knew that, what he now was, was "God's workmanship," not his own doing. He was aware that to be "created," meant "to be made out of nothing." That is, when God started on Paul he had nothing to work with. Such words of humility made the apostle's teaching on reconciliation palatable to those ready to respond to such grace. No one is turned-on to the gospel by a proclaimer who is sensed to be a conceited egotist.

It is not only God who says, "I hate pride and arrogance" (Prov. 8:13). It is not alone the preacher Jeremiah who needs the advice, "Hear and pay attention, do not be arrogant, for the LORD has spoken" (13:15). All believers need to be reminded that "the LORD detests all the proud of heart" (Prov. 16:5) and he classifies with the heathen any who are "arrogant and boastful" (Rom. 1:30).

Mark my word, we need to mark our words as we present the doctrine. Do our words convey the correct message that we are saved by God's goodness and not our own? Does the listener catch the truth that, if God was open to us, we are open to accept any who humbly desire to discover and do his will? "Blessed is the man who makes the LORD his trust, who does not look to the proud" (Psa. 40:4). A preacher "wise in his own eyes" (Prov. 26:5) may not have gained enough respect in the eyes of others that they will consider his words. Elders over God's flock must be mature, lest they "become conceited and fall under the same judgment as the devil" (I Tim. 3:6). Every man's "boasting of what he has and does — comes not from the Father but from the world" (I John 2:16).

An instructor in communications, speech or homiletics will sometimes make a video of the student speaking. When that individual hears and sees himself, he or she is often surprised at what his gestures, body-language or tone of voice conveyed that was not intended. Have your words had the right tone to speak of God's amazing grace and incredible love?

TEST YOUR HEART

We are discussing Christian unity, but we cannot do that effectively without life renewal. Changing my words will flow from changing my inner thought. Jesus was right, as usual, when he observed that "from within, out of men's hearts come evil . . . arrogance and folly" (Mark 7:21-22).

Let the Great Physician examine your attitude. Has "the pride of your heart . . . deceived you" (Obad. 3)? You and I need this testing, because "a man's pride brings him low" (Prov. 29:23). In addition to this bad effect on ourselves, egocentrism has an evil consequence on our flock. In the church "pride only breeds quarrels" (Prov. 13:10) and quarrels are the raw materials out of which our adversary builds another separating wall between brethren.

Christ will turn our world upside down once we, his church, are transformed inside out. The Psalmist said of the haughty, "pride is their necklace" (73:6). It can be more a noose by which we hang ourselves. Let us "rebuke the arrogant" (Psa. 119:21).

Let us not forget that "Haughty eyes and a proud heart, the lamp of the wicked, are sin!" (Prov. 21:4). Let us daily remind ourselves that "God opposes the proud but gives grace to the humble" (James 4:6). Whatever else is an ingredient to unity, one's attitude is a basic ingredient the Lord can use to produce the oneness he desires.

9

UNITY AND THE PERIL OF NAMES

There is an old melodrama, "The Perils of Pauline." A dictionary will call that "melodramatic" which intensifies sentiment and exaggerates emotion. Such an adjective does not fit the Bible's Pauline concern regarding the peril of dividing Christ's followers by the use of party names. The apostle Paul finds it evidence that the Corinthian church was "still worldly . . . acting like mere men" in the use of party cries, such as " 'I follow Paul' . . . 'I follow Apollos' " (I Cor. 3:3-4).

If you do not think that the labels we wear make a difference, read again I Corinthians. The name above all names is the name into which we were baptized (1:13-15). Donald Guthrie is certainly correct when he takes the slogan "I follow Christ" as "Paul's own corrective comment."[1] Glorying in Christ is right. Glorying in men is wrong. It is very possible that the Corinthians were not rallying around the personalities Paul, Apollos or Cephas, but men of their own congregation. Paul wrote, "I have used myself and Apollos above as an illustration" (I Cor. 4:6, Phillip's Translation).

When the teller at the bank reminds you that you forgot to endorse your check, you learn that names do make a difference. You already knew that, for you would much rather be called a Christian than a thief or a murderer. Call a man by a good name and you bring out the best in him. Call him by a bad name and the worst will come out. To denominate something is to name it. What is your denomination? Dare you say that one is as good as another? How about "one wife is as good as another?"

NAMES THAT DIVIDE

A four year old asked her playmate, "What abomination do you belong to?" Is the wearing of party names, really that abominable? Is not the age-old adage nearer the truth that "sticks and stones may break your bones, but names will never hurt me?" The truth radiates from the pages of the New Testament that sectarian names hurt Christ, hurt God and hurt the church.

Names are used to highlight differences. That is their only purpose. To stop designating differences and to start wearing the common name Christian is to contribute greatly to the church's oneness. Paul began his unity plea, "I appeal to you, brothers, in the name of our Lord Jesus Christ" (1:10). That name was a direct condemnation of the various party names being used in Corinth. Unscriptural names do divide. The common name Christian adheres to the Savior of all. It is patronymic. Denominational names point to institutional differences.

An old tract by Walter E. Stram still makes sense. Hear the opening paragraph:

When you were married your wife gladly accepted your name. How would you feel and act if some night when you came home from work your wife would inform you that she has decided to drop your name, and start wearing the name of the neighbor man? Would you smile back at her, and reply, "That's alright, Honey, because there really is nothing in a name anyway"? I can't imagine your being that sweet and peaceable. You would probably tell her, "Lady, if you're going to live under my roof, you'll have to wear my name." Suppose your name is Smith. You wouldn't even compromise, and allow her to call herself Mrs. Jones-Smith, or Mrs. Brown-Smith. If she would as much as suggest dropping your name, or even hyphenating it, in favor of another man's name, you certainly would question her love for you. But, what respectable loving bride would ever want to forsake her husband's name, and wear the name of another man?

Today men wear the name of John the Baptist, Calvin, Wesley or Luther. "What after all, is Apollos? And what is Paul? Only servants, through whom you came to believe" (I Cor. 3:5). Others define themselves by forms of church government, calling themselves Congregationalists, Episcopalians or Presbyterians. The members throughout the week generally go about their business giving little attention to their denominational particularities as they mingle with other believers. But let Sunday come and the church professionals polarize their group, where it is made aware of those things which divide. Have your neighbors in for a Bible study and note how one they all feel around God's Word. All who belong to Christ, belong to all the others who belong to him. Focus on Christ and oneness follows. Call attention to denominational distinctions and the enjoyed harmony begins to dissolve.

The *Reader's Digest* had the short quip contributed by Alfred L. Prosser. It went like this:

> She was sick in bed, and her husband, who was fixing her a cup of tea, called out that he couldn't find the tea. "I don't know what could be easier to find," she answered. "It's right on the front of the pantry shelf in a cocoa tin marked matches!"

Our sick world is at the terrible disadvantage in finding Jesus, its only hope, for his story is hidden behing titles, meaningless to the man in the street.

Is it not confusing to ask a convert in Northern China to become a Southern Baptist? Is it not muddying the waters of baptism to ask if we then entered the Church of Christ (instrumental), or the Church of Christ (vocal music only)? The book of Acts tells of persons accepting salvation "in Jerusalem, and in all Judea and Samaria, and to the ends of the earth" (1:8) and not one of them had heard of Luther or Wesley. Neither did they become a part of Roman Catholicism nor Protestant Denominationalism. None were "baptized into the name" (I Cor. 1:13) of any man. For "into" (εἰς) implies entrance into fellowship with and allegiance to Christ, not to a segment of his body or to a vantage point of theology.

When someone asks you what you are, tell the truth. Acknowledge Christ. Call yourself a Christian. A druggist hangs out his sign, John Doe, Druggist. An attorney puts on his door, James Brown, Lawyer. Put out your shingle, Your Name, Christian. You are in the King's business. Don't hide it. The television sales-pitch, "Try it. You'll like it," is appropriate here. For if you will be only a Christian — no hyphenation, like "Presbyterian-Christian" or "Fundamentalist-Christian" — I guarantee you'll like it, God will like it, and the neighbors will appreciate it too. Wear Christ's name, share Christ's name and bear Christ's name to others. The sooner we forget the party names, the sooner we'll forget the differences that divide. We have no monopoly on the name Christian, making it include but a few million people. That would be as misleading as to fill a bath-tub with water and call it the ocean.

NAMES THAT UNITE

Any mathematician will tell you that fractions can be added together by finding the "common denominator." Any churchman can realize that adding Presbyterian, Baptist, Adventist, Christian, etc. will require finding the "common denomination" or name big enough to unite the fractions. $\frac{1}{2} + \frac{1}{4} + \frac{1}{8}$ requires that eight be recognized as the common denominator (i.e. $\frac{4}{8}$ + $\frac{2}{8}$ + $\frac{1}{8}$). Presbyterians are not Baptists, nor are Catholics Protestants. Yet each claims to be Christian. Leaving other issues yet unresolved, the name Christian is seen to be the only nomenclature great enough to be all-inclusive.

Billy Sunday exalted the name of Jesus Christ, saying, "There is no name like His. It is more inspirational than Caesar's, it is more musical than Beethoven's, it is more conquering than Napoleon's, it is more eloquent than Demosthenes!" Wearing his name signifies our relationship to him. The party names are to be avoided because they hide that relationship under a cloud.

I understand the "new name that the mouth of the LORD" would bestow (Isa. 62:2) to be the name "Christian (given) first at Antioch" (Acts 11:26). The passage in Greek contains three infinitives, which are subordinate to the main verb of the sentence. Paul and Barnabas are said to have "met with the church . . . taught great numbers" and to have called the disciples Christians. This is a summary by Luke of the workers' activities in Antioch. The "disciples" in the sentence, being in the accusative case, is the object of the verb "called," not the subject. The preachers "called" the believers Christians. That term "called" in every other New Testament instance is a designation for God's action.[2] This "new name that the mouth of the LORD will bestow," came as the nations began to see his righteousness and kings his glory, as Isaiah had predicted. Antioch was the first Gentile church.

The name Christian has unmistakable significance. To be called a President, King, Emperor or Czar carries no moral or ethical connotation. But, when your peers say, "There is a Christian indeed," the highest honor has been paid you. You are recognized as one who belongs to Christ and walks his way. John Cumming, a minister of the Scottish National Church in London, England around the middle of the nineteenth century, observed:

The first name, pronounced from heaven, was "Christian"; and we may depend upon it, it will be the last; for just in proportion as we grow toward the beautiful original in character, in the same proportion will those assumed human names — "Presbyterians," "Independents," "Baptists," "Episcopalians," "Churchmen," "Dissenters" — drop off. Just as Christ is in a Christian heart, all and in all, so, when that inner influence becomes an outer life, "Christian" will be in a Christian's vocabulary, all and in all, also.[3]

If you call yourself a Lutheran, would you consider this. "Lutheran" means a follower of Luther, as surely as "Christian" means a follower of Christ. Are you really following Luther? He said,

I pray you leave my name alone and do not call yourselves Lutherans but Christians. Who is Luther? My doctrine is not mine. I have not been crucified for anyone. St. Paul would not permit that anyone should call themselves of Paul, nor of Peter, but of Christ. How, then, does it befit me, a miserable bag of dust and ashes, to give my name to the children of Christ. Cease, my dear friends, to cling to these party names and distinctions. Away with them all; let us call ourselves only "Christian" after him from whom our doctrine comes.[4]

The way to show respect for the reformer Luther is to follow his good advice at this point. Why wear the name of a servant, when the name of your Master is available.

Mr. Methodist, have you considered the possibility that the individual history-books claim as the founder of Methodism, pleads with those under his influence to be simply Christian? He expressed:

I would to God that all party names and unscriptural phrases and forms which have divided the Christian world were forgot; that we might all agree to sit down together as humble loving disciples at the feet of a common Master, to hear his word, to imbibe his Spirit, and to transcribe his life into our own.[5]

If Lutherans have thus-far failed to follow Luther on the name to be worn, will Wesleyans fail to follow Wesley?

For another example from the denominational world, let us hear from a Baptist. Historians know that records of older Baptist churches in America called themselves churches of Christ. M. P. Hunt, Field Secretary of the Southern Baptist Convention, told its national gathering in Kansas City, Missouri on June 9, 1904, "In the records of all our older churches will be found the name, 'The Church of Christ.' " I challenge you to visit Moscow in the Soviet Union today and ask where "the Baptists" meet. As you enter, note the name inscribed on the building. Yes, it is Church of Christ.

Dr. Hinson, addressing the General Convention of Northern Baptists at Cleveland, Ohio, on May 19 of 1904, spoke, "I sometimes feel sorry that the word 'Baptist,' which was flung at us by our enemies and stuck, should be our name, for often its accent of an act obscures to others our great mission to the world. Perhaps yet we will go back to the name, 'Christian.' " Add to his testimony that of the noted Charles Hadden Spurgeon, preaching in Exeter Hall in London. He said, "I look forward with pleasure to the day when there will not be a Baptist living. I hope they will soon be gone. I hope the 'Baptist' name will soon perish, but let Christ's name last forever."[6]

A small boy returning from an inter-denominational meeting asked his parents, "Why is it they always talk about John the Baptist, but never mention Jesus the Presbyterian?"[7] Not only little boys get confused over party-labels. The Presbyterian, Albert Barnes, affirmed "These divisions should be merged into the holy name Christian." George Arthur Buttrick, agreed, "It is not my job to make the world Presbyterian or yours to make it Methodist. Our united job, under God, is to make the world Christian." Henry Ward Beecher once said at the communion table, "Let me speak the language of heaven and call you simply 'Christians.' "

When some of the Congregational Christian Churches and the Evangelical and Reformed Church merged into a new United Church of Christ in 1957, S.S. Lappin of Bedford, Indiana wrote the Editor of the Christian Evangelist (the November 25, 1957 issue) asking, "Was it not but the formation of a new denomination, with a slightly less partisan name . . . the adoption of a new name, though it be a better name, does not change the character of the thing named. This highlights the truth that Bible names must be accompanied by Bible definitions. Church of Christ or Disciples of Christ must not be terms applied to a few "in Christ" but to all the redeemed.

This admission in no way lessens the need to return to Bible names, it only insists that we should use Bible names for Bible realities. When a little girl told her mother that she wanted to change her name, the parent replied, "Do you not love your mother, your father and your brothers? If you wear a different name, people will think you belong to someone else."

> O Wondrous name! which God has given
>   For saints on earth to wear,
> Uniting them with Christ in heaven,
>   Whose joys they hope to share.
>
> Deny that name! How could I, Lord!
>   'Twould make me blush with shame,
> Nay, though a thousand Plinys ask,
>   My answer is the same.
>
> A Christian, yes, a Christian, sir;
>   'Tis all I hope to be;
> No other name shall ere supplant
>   The name Christ gave to me.
>
> When at the sacred altar shrine
>   He took me as His bride,
> And said, "I'm yours, in life, in death;
>   Keep ever near my side,"
>
> Then blame me not, my pilgrim friends,
>   When I refuse to wear
> A human name, since that of Christ,
>   Is mine to have and share. [8]

Whatever your religious upbringing, let there be "no more boasting about men! All things are yours, whether Paul or Apollos or Cephas or the world or life or death or the present or the future — all are yours, and you are of Christ, and Christ is of God" (I Cor. 3:21-23). All the great teachers of the gospel and all the great facts of that gospel belong to all believers for all time and eternity. Learn of Christ from Paul and Apollos, Augustine and Aquinas, Luther and Campbell. Serve under presbyters, baptize believers and be methodical in what you do, but that will not make you a Presbyterian-Baptist-Methodist. It will but demonstrate you are a Christian in name, but not name only.

It is not an easy assignment nor a task uncostly to give up a name that goes back in your family's tradition. Doing the right thing is seldom easy. Helping answer Jesus' prayer for his family's oneness has its price. But isn't the Baptist Russell Conwell near the truth when he proclaimed, "The time has come in the history of the church when God says, 'Unite! Unite!' God is calling us to 'Unite! Unite!' I would not for the world forsake my denomination, but for Christ's sake I would gladly give it up forever!"

"For this reason I kneel before the Father, from whom his whole family in heaven and on earth derives its name" (Eph. 3:14). Let party names perish. Let Jesus Christ be all in all.

Endnotes

1. The *New Bible Commentary* (Grand Rapids: Wm. B. Eerdmans Publishing Company, 1970), p. 1054.
2. Matthew 2:12,22; Luke 2:26; Acts 10:22; Romans 7:3; Hebrews 8:5; 11:7; 12:25.
3. John Cummings, *The Daily Life*, p. 262.
4. Stork, *Life of Luther*, p. 289.
5. Quoted in *Hardeman's Tabernacle Sermons, Volume V*, p. 60.
6. *Spurgeon Memorial Library, Volume I*, p. 168.
7. Harold M. Mallett in "Save the Union Meeting," Church Management, May, 1955.
8. Author unknown.

10

UNITY AND THE PUSHING OF OPINIONS

The symbol of division is a wall. The Berlin Wall for too many years forced a divided Germany. Iron curtains, bamboo curtains or religious-opinion curtains make unnatural separations of people who ought to be together. We have found Satan to be behind church schism in every place and at every time. Often the fences he erects are based on human pride or party labels. At other times the barbed wire, keeping God's sheep apart, is not divine revelation but human opinion. Humans would not be human, as God made them, if they did not have opinions. That which makes opinions divisive, is that the enemy of the soul entices a man to force his opinion on all other brothers and sisters.

To overcome that evident evil the slogan appeared, "In essentials unity, In non-essentials liberty; In all things charity." Rupertus Meldenius, sometimes known as Peter Meiderlin, wrote the words in a 1626 tract: *"In necessariis unitas; In dubiis libertus; In omnibus caritas."* The words have passed on to us through

Christian leaders such as John Bergius, Richard Baxter and Thomas Campbell.

No one can object to the words of the slogan, but the rub comes when each individual makes his own list of essentials to be distinguished from what is seemed properly to be labeled opinion. The reformer Luther held that anything not forbidden in Scripture could remain in the church of his time. His sixteenth century fellow-reformer, Zwingli, insisted that everything must be put out of the church that is not taught in the Scripture. The issue came to a head. Are the silences of Scripture, prohibitive or permissive? It is easy to see that what Christ forbids is evil and what he commands is necessary. But is there an area neither condemned nor commanded, where the Lord allows his followers to use their own good judgment? Is there a place for different opinions to be allowed, as long as they do not divide? Or is there only black or white on every issue? The gospel must never be compromised. Yet believers in the gospel can so multiply their own list of essentials that a legalism worse than Phariseeism can spring up. The Pharisees in Jesus' day so reacted against the scepticism of the Sadducees that they elevated the traditions of the elders to a position as high as the law of God.

Can we restate the old slogan, "In men's 'essentials' liberty, in God's 'opinions' unity?" If God's view on an issue is revealed to men in Scripture, we are either obedient children or rebellious sons. But what is not that clear in Scripture, even though important to me, must not be forced on a fellow believer when his mind is not so persuaded by what I call evidence. The commission of Christ calls on us to make disciples of Jesus, but I am no where sent to make disciples for my opinions out of those disciples of Christ.

IN MEN'S "ESSENTIALS" LIBERTY

The great commission allows great *permission*, when it comes to how we carry out Christ's orders. Mark 16:15 begins, "Go into

114

all the world." Train, plane, car, boat or foot allow alternate ways of getting to a destination for preaching the gospel. In that command no deviation is allowed, but method of travel is a human preference. It is not right for those who prefer riding the train to consider those who go by bus to be unfaithful.

The imperative of our Lord is to baptize. To *cheize* (pour) or to *rantize* (sprinkle) would not be to *baptize* (immerse) but to substitute another action for the one the King ordered. Yet the silence of the text allows for the water to be in a standing pool or running stream. The silence of the passage gives freedom to immerse the convert backward or forward. The Messiah's instruction to his representatives regarding these newly baptized believers was "teaching them to obey everything I have commanded you" (Matt. 28:20). You may teach by using an overhead, filmstrips, drama or blackboard. Method is not specified, only what is to be taught. Unity remains intact when all of us teach what Jesus commanded. You, using the teaching style most appropriate for you, and I, using a different method more effective for me, is not threatening to our oneness. But, when I question your commitment to Christ and his cause because you follow a different pedagogical style, I have rent our fellowship. Having an opinion or preference is not divisive, but pushing it as the only acceptable view or method can be.

Romans 14 stands as a flashing beacon to warn us that God expects us to tolerate differences in the family. The issue under discussion is not the toleration of evil. What the Bible defines as sin is not to be redefined as a different but acceptable life-style. Sin is sin! But there are matters, innocent in themselves, that are considered by some to be inappropriate. Paul illustrates regarding diet and days. If a person's "faith is weak" and he thinks it wrong to eat meat, the Christian is to "accept" the weak brother, "not look down on him." Even though God has freed us from the Levitical food regulations, he has not made us executioners of those uninformed of their full freedom in Christ. "The man who eats everything must not look down on him who does not, and the man who does not eat every thing must not condemn the man who does, for God has accepted him" (Rom. 14:3). Those last four words are a marvel of grace. As wrong doctrinally as the person under discussion, "God has accepted him." To do less is not grace, but a disgrace. "Food does not bring us near to God; we are no worse if we do not eat, and no better if we do" (I Cor. 8:8).

Holy days and holidays fill one man's agenda of observances. Another individual "considers every day alike" (Rom.14:5). Debates and arguments have their place in explaining "the way of God more adequately" (Acts. 18:26), but the attitude that excommunicates the untaught has no place in the religion of God's unmerited favor. We ever need to ask, "Why do you judge your brother? Or why do you look down on your brother?" (Rom. 14:10).

If salvation is only bestowed on those Christians who are 100% orthodox on every topic, the "Father's house" in eternity will not need the "many rooms" (John 14:2) Jesus went to prepare. A small single room will be more than adequate. Rejoice with me that our salvation is based on God's goodness, not mine; and our acceptance in Christ's church is based on our following the perfect pattern even when we do not follow it perfectly.

An opinion is only an opinion. It ought not be elevated to an essential. F. G. Allen in *New Testament Christianity* says, "What God has clearly expressed as his will, men should be required to accept and do. . . . Further than this we cannot go without requiring unity of opinion; and that the Bible does not teach."[1] Allen had caught the spirit of Thomas Campbell's *Declaration and Address*, where it is written:

> Where no express law is, there can be no formal, no intentional transgression, even although its implicit and necessary consequences had forbid the thing, had they been discovered. Upon the whole, we see one thing is evident: the Lord will bear with the weaknesses, the involuntary ignorances, and mistakes of his people, though not with their presumption.

116

As early as 1837, Alexander, the son of Thomas Campbell, put out a red flare for the readers of the *Millennial Harbinger*. It was on the danger of elevating our opinions to the status of matter of faith. He wrote:

> Unless this matter is better understood, it will fare with us as with . . . other religious communities. We shall be broken to pieces as well as they. It is conceded that we have the right to form our own opinions, and to express them when asked to do so under proper auspices; but this is very different from the right to propagate our speculations instead of preaching and practicing the precepts of the Gospel.

That prophecy of trouble down the line for advocates of the Restoration Plea, if they failed to distinguish essentials and opinions, sadly came to pass. Winfred E. Garrison, a church historian of that movement, blamed some unfortunate separations in that tradition on the "mis-labeling of opinions as indisputable revelations." He added, "Those who continue to forge the name of God to their own inferences, opinions and programs, will go on being intolerant separatists and sectarians."[2]

For unity to prevail the personal conscience of each individual must be respected and protected by those holding other views. Potential little denominations can arise over pushing the opinion that this particular Christian college is best, or that Christian periodical is superior, or this missionary is most loyal. One's opinion, as to the truest publishing house or the most exemplary large congregation, must not be the sun around which a new sect begins to orbit. My ego is not king. Christ is King! Harmony is the goal. Rivalry is not the way. "Whatever you believe about these things keep between yourself and God" (Rom. 14:22).

IN GOD'S "OPINIONS" UNITY

My opinions are my private property, but God's "opinions" (if

117

we may call the Lord's revelation such) are public property and belong to all Christians. The church is composed of many members and each member has his opinions. But that church has one head who has revealed its one, divinely-given faith. That "faith was once for all entrusted to the saints" (Jude 3). Be careful to observe that this revelation was not for one saint, nor one segment of saints, but for all who are saints. The plural noun is not meant to speak of a few now living in Utah, nor a smaller number so canonized after death by Rome. It refers to the entire church.

Henry Knox Sherill, a former president of the National Council of the Churches of Christ in the United States, observed, "The trouble with the church is that too many people have great convictions about little things. They fail to grasp the majesty that confronts them." This sharp distinction between the comparatively small issues over which believers hotly debate and the awesome gospel that unites us is the matter before us. Men's opinions are of little consequence. GOD'S OPINIONS — his Word revealed in flesh and in writing — has eternal issue.

In Alexander Campbell's *Christian System* the matter is clearly expressed:

> The belief of one fact, and that upon the best evidence in the world, is all that is requisite, as far as faith goes, to salvation. This belief of this one fact, and submission to one institution expressive of it, is all that is required of heaven to admission into the church. . . . The one fact is expressed in a single proposition — that Jesus the Nazarene is the Messiah . . . the one institution is Baptism into the name of the Father, and of the Son, and of the Holy Spirit.[3]

To Campbell "faith in Christ and obedience to him (is) the only test of Christian character, and the only bond of church union, communion, and co-operation."[4]

Circumstances of the time in which the apostles lived led to some actions that are not of the very essence of the church. Greetings with a kiss or washing feet were expressions of love and hospitality throughout Palestine and much of their world at that time. But the atonement for sin accomplished at Calvary and the conquering of death by Jesus' bodily resurrection are the heart and core of Christianity. Customs of men may vary from culture to culture and age to age, but the redeeming gospel of Christ is eternal. The former are indifferent. The latter are essential. The first are options. The last are tests of fellowship because they inseparably relate to the gospel.

The Paul who argued for variations of opinion in Romans 14, insisted on unanimity of faith in Galatians 1. "If anybody is preaching to you a gospel other than what you accepted, let him be eternally condemned!" (1:9). In words ever as strong, John, Peter, Jude and the rest strike a death blow against those who "deny Jesus Christ our only Sovereign and Lord" (Jude 4). The sacred, never to be tampered with, is the gospel, its facts, its promises, its commands and its warnings.

Extraneous and even ridiculous opinions can be endured for a time, but these prejudices of weak brethren do not, or ought not, break our fellowship. Infraction of the faith, trampling "the Son of God under foot" or treating "as an unholy thing the blood of the covenant" (Heb. 10:29), is another matter. Our goal as church is not unanimity in opinions, but oneness in the essential truth. We can disagree in the non-essentials without being disagreeable. We must agree in the essential that Christ is Lord and his gospel is truth.

Where denominational segments have some teaching or practice that they stress, the apostolic church stressed the gospel and its Christ. Z. T. Sweeney, addressing adherents of the call to restore the faith and practice of first century Christianity, preached on the question, "Have We Outgrown Our Plea?" In that message he put his finger on the pulse of that unity effort of his day declaring, "We have but *one peculiarity*, and that lies in the fact that *we have no peculiarities*."[1] The genius of that great body was in seeing that the gospel universals unite, while a tradition's particulars can divide. Everyone has a right to his or her opinions, but pushing, shoving or pressing them on others leads to splits. Every Christian has the need of total commitment to Christ's gospel. That they all have "received." In that they have all taken their "stand." By that each will be "saved" (I Cor. 15:2).

Endnotes

1. Z. T. Sweeny, Editor Volume II, (Columbus, Indiana: New Testament Christianity Book Fund, Incorporated, 1930), p. 249.

2. From a sermon, "A Fork in the Road," delivered at the 1964 Pension Fund Minister's Breakfast in Detroit, Michigan at the International Convention of Disciples of Christ.

3. (Bethany, Virginia, January 2, 1835), p. 101.

4. *Ibid.*, p. x.

5. *New Testament Christianity, Volume III*, ibid., p. 83.

11

UNITY AND THE PERVERSION OF CREEDS

Christianity is a faith. Its followers are called "believers" (Acts 5:12). How then can a creed be listed as one of the devil's dividing walls of separation? Why would a unity movement rising in nineteenth century North America be looked on as non-creedal?

A careful look at the slogans used by reformers in the tradition of Barton Stone or Thomas and Alexander Campbell did not say, "No creed." It was rather "No creed but Christ." The objection was to the substitution of human creedal statements for what was divinely given.

"Credo" is but the Latin for "I believe." The church, from its earliest days, preached its convictions and confessed its faith daily. Those, who in our day seek to return to the faith and practice of the church of apostolic times, object to substituting man-made creedal systems that replace Christ and his revealed teaching. A personal expression of my understanding of Scripture, orally or in

121

writing, is in order; but exalting that understanding into an authoritative creed for all others in Christ's church is to blow it out of all proportion.

A personal statement of faith is one thing. A doctrinal statement, to be used with ecclesiastical force to measure your fitness for church fellowship is another. In church history the creeds, such as Nicean or Chalcedonian, or the confessions of faith, like the Westminister or the Augsburg, were meant to be more than *testimonies of faith*. Their intentions were to be *tests of faith*. The confessional statements became exclusionary statements. Those framing the historic creeds considered the stated articles of faith as essential to salvation, or at least, basic to the well-being of the church. In an article on "Creeds and Unity," written by Winfred Ernest Garrison for *The Christian Evangelist* of July 19, 1950, it was said,

> The most objectionable feature of creeds . . . is their assumption of inerrancy and unchangeableness. To be sure, creeds have been revised. But the possibility of future revision is never contemplated when a creed is adopted. If it were tentative and reformable, it could not be authoritative. No creed contains an article providing a method for its amendment.[1]

THE EXCLUSIVE CREEDS

The body of Christ has suffered, not from the hardening of the arteries — that affliction that human bodies often suffer — but by what one has called the hardening of the categories. When authoritative human creeds arose they required acceptance of all points for remaining in the fellowship. Ecclesiastical carpenters went to building theological fences to keep some brothers out. To again quote from Garrison:

> Eusebius' first draft for a creed at Nicaea, which was largely in phraseology quoted directly from the New Testament, was re-

jected because it would not exclude the Arians. What was wanted was not a creed that said what the New Testament said — for even the Arians would accept that — but one which said what the orthodox thought the New Testament meant.[2]

The commission of Christ is to communicate to all, but not to excommunicate at all.

Will unity be any closer if we travel the creedal route of unity by exclusion and compulsion? Since human creeds of the past ejected some members of the church and served as strong doors to keep certain believers in Christ from entrance, will new or revised creeds do better in the future? Alexander Campbell in his 1843 debate with the Presbyterian N. L. Rice affirmed that "human creeds, as bonds of union and communion, are necessarily heretical and schismatical." His case rested in the foundation that fallible human opinion must never be substituted for divine revelation. If I accept all the Scriptures say about Jesus, how can other Christians reject me as heretic if I cannot grasp with my mind their theological definitions and philosophical distinctions in technical language? Can children no longer have a place in the community of believers? Would only those living as long as Methuselah and having the brain of an Einstein be able to affirm, with no fingers crossed, "I believe every word as expressed by the council in its majority vote?" How can the creeds of men, made by so few, be imposed on the many who love and desire to follow Christ? Is unity in Christ ours only after reaching a certain level of understanding?

W. F. Lown, in an address at the Seventh Annual Consultation of the Internal Unity of the Christian Churches, stated that "the unity of Christians should be a *result* of Christian commitment and ministry, and not an elusive *goal* after which ecclesiastics scamper with theological butterfly nets." Someone defined a human creed as "a string of metaphysical propositions conceived in a scholastic brain and put into scholastic phraseology." Rather than a heart-thrilling, life-altering confession of faith, some creeds could more accurately be called a "confusion of faith."

Many, after reading through the fine-line distinctions of a historic creed, may feel with Abraham Lincoln:

> I have never united myself to any church, because I have found difficulty in giving my assent, without mental reservation, to the long, complicated statements of Christian doctrine which characterize their articles of belief and confession of faith.[3]

If not sympathizing with Lincoln, one might yet feel with the lady pressed on a theological matter, who responded, "If you want to know what I believe, you go talk to my Rector." Too many who recite their creed neither know what it means nor believe what it says. Churchmen are tempted to hypocrisy, reciting words they do not inwardly accept. Test that by listening to denominational preachers whose liturgies affirm truths that their seminary studies have washed out of them.

Another strike against creedalism is that it substitutes human words to guard the truth of the gospel for the divinely given Scripture which is adequate to that grand task of protecting the Christian message. Those evangelicals who insist that creeds are essential to protecting orthodoxy butt their heads against the New Testament assurance that "all Scripture . . . is useful for teaching, rebuking, correcting and training in righteousness, so that the man of God may be thoroughly equipped" (II Tim. 3:16-17). "Thoroughly equipped" are words of adequacy. In a court-room scene of long ago, an Irishman was asked if he had spoken truth, the whole truth and nothing but truth. His answer, "Yes, your honor, and then some," reminds me of some creedal traditions in their going beyond divine revelation.

When Hollywood's Paramount Studios envisioned the movie "The Ten Commandments," Cecile B. DeMille listened to the speeches by General Van Fleet with a view of using the General's voice for the voice of God. Before and after that date in our century, men have tried out for that role. "*Vox populi, vox dei*" is never true. The voice of the people is not and never has been the voice of God. The majority is seldom right. If it were, rock music would prove better than Beethoven, and taverns might win over churches. Not even the voice of church people can be compared with the word of the Almighty. "Thus saith the preacher" — or creed or some convention resolution — can never supersede "thus saith the Lord." At best a human creed is incomplete, substituting partial truth for God's full self-disclosure. Creeds displace the Christian Scriptures, add to the Scriptures or omit from the Scriptures. They never are the same as the Bible. Often their wording is not the more simple, non-technical language of inspired authors but the religious vocabulary of theological clergymen. The metaphysical speculations of later centuries almost hide the beauty of the religion Jesus propounded in his lovely parables and simple sermons.

How can it be insisted that creeds are essential to the church's being or well-being, when the church existed in essence before any of them were formed? Why should a formulation of words created in the 4th Century by a turbulent church council at the command of a Roman Emperor be accepted as final or perfect? The church on the pages of Acts was welded together by its warm conviction that Jesus was Lord and not frozen together by the rigid phrases of extra-congregational superiors. No less than Emil Brunner exposed the folly of finding doctrinal security in our creeds rather than God's Bible. He wrote:

The living Word of God is secured — and the same time replaced — by theology and dogma; the fellowship is secured — and re-placed — by the institution; faith, which proves its reality by love, is secured-and-replaced — by a creed and a moral code.[4]

A unity based on any single creedal statement or a combination of many will only result in unity among those whose consciences accept that creed and separation from those who do not. Is there a better way?

125

THE INCLUSIVE CREED

The Restoration Movement advocates suggested this alternate route to unity:

Let the BIBLE be substituted for all human creeds; FACTS, for definitions; THINGS, for words; FAITH, for speculation; UNITY OF FAITH, for unity of opinion; THE POSITIVE COMMAND-MENTS OF GOD, for human legislation and tradition; PIETY, for ceremony; MORALITY, for partisan zeal; THE PRACTICE OF RELIGION, for the mere profession of it: and the work is done.[5]

The prospective convert you meet on the pages of the New Testament was never handed a list of propositional sentences to be affirmed. The convert was confronted with that person sent from God. The Messiah was to be trusted with all one's being. "I know whom I have believed," wrote Paul near the end of his ministry (II Tim. 1:12). The object of his faith was the person of Christ. His faith, like all other Christians you meet in the Scripture accounts, was a warm human trust in Jesus. The believer's uniting faith centered in Christ, the God-man, not in religious propositions filled with non-biblical terms. Theories about his person did not usurp the believer's time from obedience to his will. Complicated theological explanations were not the basis of their trust. They knew enough about their human condition to realize that they were lost and they had total confidence that Jesus was the hoped for Messiah, God's Son, their Savior and Lord. Their faith was not in some written creed but in the living Christ. Common allegiance to him was their bond of unity.

I, just the other Sunday evening, enjoyed a panel of four preachers speaking of marriage. Each of the speakers had not only preached the gospel for over fifty years, they also had been married more than half a century. Claude Guild pointed to the secret of lasting happy marriages by quoting the line of an old hymn, "Speak Them Over Again to Me, Wonderful Words of

Life." He encouraged young couples often to speak the words that put life into a marriage — words such as "I trust you," "I'm committed to you," "I believe in you," or "You can do it." The "wonderful words" that bring harmony to the church and life to a believer are not lines of recited creeds in liturgy, but the heart realization "Jesus loves me," "He died for me," "He rose again," "He's coming back," and "I am his."

When Dwight L. Moody was responding to questions put to him in London by leading clergymen, one asked, "What's your creed, Mr. Moody?" His quick retort was, "My creed's in print." When pressed where to find it, he quietly said, "Isaiah fifty-three, five." That Biblical confession reads, "he was pierced for our transgressions, he was crushed for our iniquities; the punishment that brought us peace was upon him, and by his wounds we are healed."

Peter worded his faith in Jesus, "You are the Christ, the Son of the living God" (Matt. 16:16) and John stated his conviction was that "Jesus is the Christ the Son of God" (John 20:31). Thomas called him, "My Lord and my God" (John 20:28). Paul affirmed, "Jesus Christ is Lord" (Phil. 2:11). Each would have said "Amen" to the wording the other had used. The point is that every "good confession" (I Tim. 6:13) is the expression of total confidence in the person Jesus of Nazareth. Those witnesses as to who Jesus is were freely given and fully believed.

Just as the unity in Roman Catholicism with all its diversity is held together by allegiance to one person — the pope of Rome — the oneness of the first century church was made a reality by commitment to the one person — Jesus, God's Son, the only Savior. The catacombs of Rome reveal the sign of the fish and its logo as testimony that everyone confessed the good confession. The word for "fish" (ἰχθύς) served as an acrostic for "Jesus, Christ, God's Son, Savior" (Ιησοῦς Χριστὸς Θεοῦ Υἱὸς Σωτήρ). This creed's confession was all that was required to make a convert the proper subject for baptism (Acts 8:36-38). The "one faith" confessed and the "one baptism" shared, made believers members of the "one body" (Eph. 4:4-6).

Since those early days, Christs's church has been fractured and divided by lesser loyalties to human dogmas, traditions and opinions. Going back beyond the creeds of the centuries four to twenty to the living, loving, trustful surrender to the person of Christ, as in century one, can make us one again. Our choice is to be "tragically divided and tradition choked" or to be gloriously one and Spirit filled. Cutting away the accretions of the years, like a vinedresser pruning his vines, will lead to more fruit in the future. Someone said, "If you change the formulas for gunpowder you can not get the "Boom!" Trust in Jesus produced a life-change, that mental assent to propositional sentences, however accurate, can not accomplish. Alexander Campbell explained his non-creedal approach, "We have decided to open the gates of admission to the Church as wide as the gates of heaven." The concern was not that he might let too many in, but that he might leave some out.

What must I believe to be saved? Must I have settled the millennial issue? Is the music question of instrumental accompaniment or vocal singing only prerequisite to my acceptance before God? Or is the promise still, "Everyone who believes that Jesus is the Christ is born of God" (I John 5:1,5) and "He who has the Son has life" (I John 5:12).

Join John Wesley in stating, "If your heart beats with my heart in love and loyalty to Christ, then give me your hand." Add your voice to that of John Oxenham:

> Now what, but WHOM, I do believe,
>   That in my darkest hour of need,
> Hath comfort that no mortal creed to mortal man may give.
>   Not what, but WHOM!
>   For Christ is more than all the creeds,
>   And His full life of gentle deeds
>   Shall all the creeds outlive.

Not what I do believe, but WHOM!
  WHO walks beside me in the gloom?
  WHO shares the burden wearisome?
  WHO all the dim way doth illume,
  And bids me look beyond the tomb
  That larger life to live?

Not what I do believe!
  But WHOM!
  Not WHAT,
  But WHOM![6]

Endnotes

1. p. 699.
2. *Ibid.*, p. 698.
3. Edgar Dewitt Jones, *Lincoln and the Preachers*, (New York: Hooper and Brothers, 1948), p. 141.
4. *The Misunderstanding of the Church,* (Philadelphia: Westminster Press, 1953), p. 53.
5. *The Christian System*, (Bethany, Virginia, January 2, 1835), p. 90.
6. *"Bees in Amber."*

12

UNITY AND THE PLIGHT OF MAN

The light of the world is Jesus. The plight of the world is sin. And sin separates. "Your iniquities have separated you from your God," says Isaiah (59:2). Sins also separate brothers. To what other cause can we attribute schism in the family of God? It is evident that Christ's flock is separated by human creeds, human opinions, human names and human pride. The Lord wills our oneness, while the devil rejoices at our division.

In the garden of Eden death was a promised penalty if God's law was violated. "When you eat of it you will surely die" (Gen. 2:17) were words uttered to Adam who "lived 930 years" (Gen. 5:5). How can it be said that death set in at disobedience, when over nine centuries of life followed? Pick a rose or some other flower and give it to one you love. Even putting it in water will only extend the appearance of life for a few days. Death set in at the moment of separation of the flower from the stem that bore it. Sever a finger from a hand or a toe from a foot and that member

131

cut off from the body will not live.

THE SIN OF DENOMINATIONALISM

The plight of man is sin and "the wages of sin is death" (Rom. 6:23). Death is the separation from God who is life. Our separations from one another — our divisions — when recognized as sin, is the first step in the recovery of oneness. Was Paul right in listing "discord . . . dissensions (and) factions" as "acts of the sinful nature," as surely as "debauchery" and "orgies" (Gal. 5:19-21)?

Look at the human name being worn — Paulist, Cephasite, Apollosite, Lutheran, etc. — and try to justify it in the light of James 2:9: "If you show favoritism, you sin and are convicted by the law as lawbreakers." Exalting men or methods can dethrone the One who alone has right to the high place in our hearts.

"Faith comes from hearing the message" (Rom. 10:17). Was it the message of New Testament Scripture that led to the Roman or Protestant practices prevalent in the rituals of their liturgies or the formation of their structures? If not, there needs to be heard the warning, "Everything that does not come from faith is sin" (Rom. 14:23). There is only "one Lord" (Eph. 4:5) in the "one body." And singing loudly, "Lord, Lord" will not pass muster for any who fail to do "the will of (the) Father who is in heaven" (Matt. 7:21). If pledging allegiance to a denominational system is recognized in the light of Scripture to be wrong, can we continue the perpetuation of such denominationalism and yet remain innocent? "Anyone . . . who knows the good he ought to do and doesn't do it, sins," wrote James (4:17). Who can argue that denominationalism is right? Recall that "all unrighteousness is sin" (I John 5:17, KJV). Who can establish that sectarianism is promoted in Christ's "perfect law" (James 1:25)? Keep in mind that "sin is lawlessness" (I John 3:4).

Toning down the word "sin" in regard to church division and

renaming it with some term more acceptable to our ears will not change its evil nature. Renaming alcoholism a sickness, or sodomy a divergent life-style only helps blind us to the Bible's "Thus saith the Lord." The Jewish novelist, Ludwig Lewisohn, made the astute observation, "What the people need today is moral conversion and not new names for old sins." Sin is sin and not a "harmless weakness," a "complex" or an "inhibition." Sectarianism by any other name is still sin. No sin against God dare be considered small.

The "hatred" in Paul's list of the works of the flesh in Galatians 6:19-21 is the deep-seated ill-will that shows itself in family feuds. The "discord" is the enmity that works havoc in the community of believers. The "jealousy" is that feeling of resentment that develops toward one considered a rival, threatening one's own advantage. The "fits of rage" or "wrath" (KJV) are the passionate outbursts that attend strife, even in arguments regarding some Bible doctrine. The "selfish ambitions" are the "envying" (KJV) of favor or honor desired for self but begrudged to another. The "dissensions" and "factions" that pit brother against brother are the evil results of the evil spirit of partisanship. Some one can well ask, as in the *Christian Standard* of January 21, 1990, "What would be the gain for men to leave the world where they have been fighting their enemies to come into the church and start fighting their brethren?"

THE CURE OF RECONCILIATION

Two young Catholic girls were studying for their catechism class. Boasting as to how far they were in their studies, the first bragged that she was beyond "Original Sin." The other proudly asserted, "I'm way beyond that, I'm beyond 'Redemption.' " Is today's divided Christendom beyond redemption? Certainly not! God's remedy is infallible and our need is imperative. Oren Arnold in the *Kiwanis Magazine* wrote, "What the world needs is a

133

closer agreement on what the world needs." I believe we in the church, different from the world, know our need for unity. We pray with David for "an undivided heart" (Psa. 86:11) and with Jesus for an undivided church (John 17:21).

Jesus specializes in atonement — at-one-ment. From God sin had separated us, but we were reconciled to him through the death of his Son . . . we have now received reconciliation" (Rom. 5:10-11). In Christ our estrangement from the Heavenly Father has been overcome and in Christ our relationship with our brothers can be mended. Jesus is "our peace" and he "has destroyed the barrier, the dividing wall of hostility" (Eph. 2:14). "In him all things hold together" (Col. 1:17).

Knowing that God wills our unity and that only Satan wants us divided, we must turn to Christ's teaching for the guidance we need in restoring the fellowship now broken by our sin. Broken things can be mended by the carpenter from Nazareth. All it takes is for the church to be responsive to the rasp, plane or saw of his choosing. If "your will be done on earth as it is in heaven" (Matt. 6:10) is our prayer to God, be ready to accept the ministry of gentle sand-paper or rough file. Heaven's "measuring rod" (Rev. 11:1) is the Bible. Let the work of restoration begin.

PART THREE

THE BIBLE'S DIRECTING
WORD FOR OUR GUIDANCE

13

UNITY AND THE PRIMACY OF THE TRUTH

Once we are convinced that the Lord wills our oneness and only Satan himself works for our separation from each other, we recognize our need for guidance to recover the unity God desires for His people. The Bible, as revelation from God to men, is the source where believers will find heaven's direction toward the road that leads to harmony in the church.

A train needs tracks to run on. A river of water requires banks to guide its flow toward the sea. Carpenters erecting an apartment complex must follow an architect's building plan or the structure will be chaotic in appearance and unlivable in fact. Churchmen have need of a standard by which they can distinguish a deformation from a reformation in the church. How can one be sure if a proposed change in faith or practice should be looked at as apostolic or apostate? Have we like John the Revelator been "given a reed like a measuring rod" by which to measure the temple of God and the altar (Rev. 11:1)? We know that lines must be drawn, but our desire is to draw them in the right place. We know that good will, while essential, is not enough. Scriptural unity gives high priority to the primacy of truth. Unity in truth is the path God has charted. Unity that bypasses God's revelation is a dead-end, no matter how seemingly beautiful the scenery at the early stages of the journey.

THE APPIAN WAY LEADS TO ROME

Before a congregation starts its journey toward the highly-advertised adventure to union, it would be wise to study the map God has prepared to clarify where the available roads lead. When Paul concluded his long, arduous journey to the imprisonment awaiting him in Rome, his feet followed the Appian Way (Acts 28:14-15). Is our long trek toward unity to be taken, traveling the route through Rome?

"Come home to Rome" has been, is now, and likely shall remain, the invitation extended by the Roman Catholic Church to Protestants who long for unity. The popes over the centuries have advocated unity. Considering herself the mother church, the Roman Catholic Church has left open the door for straying children to return. Admit the error of leaving, plus return to the primacy of the papacy and all will be forgiven. The Roman Catholic Church appeals that, if unity is what is longed for, then come back to where the unity is.

Thomas D. Thurman recognizes that this call to unity asks for a unity that requires "forgetting the past, forgetting convictions, forgetting the Scriptures."[1] It is a good feeling to find that after Vatican II, non-Romanists have been elevated from "heretics" to "separated brethren." Yet, does the road to Rome still lead away from Scripture? Are the gospel of Rome and the gospel of Scripture the same gospel or a different gospel? Is the submission to Christ and submission to one calling himself "the vicar of Christ" the equal obedience?

The Lord of the church taught, "No one can serve two masters" (Matt. 6:24). Following the Pope and following the Lord may be hard to do in light of the Biblical assertion that "for us there is but one God . . . and there is but one Lord, Jesus Christ" (I Cor. 8:6). To have accepted Jesus as the "one Lord" is to have deposed all other greater or lesser claimants to the throne. There were men "masquerading as apostles of Christ" (II Cor. 11:13; Rev. 2:2) in New Testament times. It should be no surprise that the practice continues into our day. Claims to apostolic succession, like all other claims, are to be tested (I Thess. 5:21. The book of Revelation spoke of some "who claim to be Jews though they are not" (3:9). This should be enough to alert us that only the naive accept every assertion of authority in speaking *ex cathedra* without putting the claimant to the X-ray test of Biblical truth.

Does your Bible call for indulgences, pilgrimages, prayers for the dead and Mariolatry? In your New Testament do you read of purgatory, holy water, the veneration of images and the sale of indulgences? What Scriptural chapter and verse calls the pope infallible, tells of praying to saints or calls the Lord's Supper "the daily sacrifice of the Mass?" How can we reconcile a Bible that teaches "A bishop then must be . . . the husband of one wife" (I Tim. 3:2) and a church that teaches only unmarried men can serve as presbyters or deacons?

Bernard Ramm, in light of the great contrast between Biblical teaching and Roman doctrine, stated that "any proposed unity of the Roman church and the Protestant bodies is not difficult, but impossible."[2] Unity by unconditional surrender to Rome is one road that could be taken. Yet, the voice at the transfiguration still can be heard and the covering cloud that hides other religious leaders still needs to do its work. The voice from heaven claimed Jesus as the one to be listened to and the cloud hid even men like Moses the lawgiver and Elijah the first of the prophets (Matt. 17:2-6; Mark 9:7-8). Following Jesus is the way to go. Following blind guides leads to falling "into a pit" (Matt. 15:14). Before raising the papal flag to flutter over the place you gather for worship, consider the other options. Edward J. Carnell in an early issue of *Christianity Today*, wrote:

> If the Reformation has done nothing else, it has clarified what is perhaps the most important theological question in this or any other age. *Do we find the truth by submitting to the church, or do we find the church by submitting to the truth?* Rome defends the first possibility, while the Reformers defend the second. [3]

THE APATHY WAY LEADS TO RESTRUCTURE

The flaming zeal of the ardent promoters of today's ecumenical movement toward union does not hide an uneasiness among the people in the pews about what is happening. A shift is taking place from the old ground of common teaching to a cohesion based on connectionalism. Some leaders among the unitists are reducing previous essentials to present indifferences. Instead of finding unity in returning to the New Testament, union is sought in compromise. Denominations get ready to give up what they like least to keep what they like most. Is joining together in social service, that even a humanist would like, going to satisfy the individual Christian who sees doctrinal convictions ignored? Oil and water can be stirred together, but will they remain permanently united? Is oneness and a mixture the same thing? Unity in depth will last. Shallow compromise will fail. Some mergers of denominations have resulted in new denominations being formed, as segments of each group have consciences that can not go along. If God has given a clear command, do churches have the option to decide if obeying or disobeying Him matters?

How can we center unity in the Lordship of Christ, if we put no meaning in the word Lord? To change another's last will and testament by erasure or addition is a fraudulent act. One who has vowed loyalty to Christ cannot at one moment say Jesus has all authority and at the next moment turn to follow practices commanded by men. A building may have the sign over the door

"United Church of Christ," but in honesty it may need to add the words, "Now under new management." Contradictions are not to be pooled. Truth and error are not to be joined together.

Kenneth Irving Brown saw tolerance as today's highly exalted virtue. But he warned:

> Tolerance is like salt. Within its limits it purifies and flavors; but in quantity it renders inedible the things it is part of. And when tolerance becomes "not caring," it makes unpalatable and destroys what it is supposed merely to flavor.[4]

A Christian, who reads his Bible regularly, finds that Christ-denying or gospel-challenging errors can not be tolerated to the undermining of revelation. Peter warned the believers, "there will be false teachers among you" (II Pet. 2:1). He illustrated the consequence of following such leaders by pointing to the Old Testament incident of Israelites that "left the straight way and wandered off" (II Pet. 2:15). John taught the necessary lesson of how the church could "recognize the Spirit of truth and the spirit of falsehood" (I John 4:6). Paul joined in clarifying that Christian tolerance did not mean tolerating "something that man made up" (Gal. 1:11). He would be the first to "praise . . . holding to the teachings, just as (he) passed them on" (I Cor. 11:2). He would be the first to admonish, "Examine yourselves to see whether you are in the faith; test yourselves" (II Cor. 13:5), affirming, "we cannot do anything against the truth, but only for the truth" (II Cor. 13:8).

One gets the impression in Scripture studies that wrongs are not to be united but eliminated. United in error is the antithesis of unity in truth. Truth is inflexible. Each individual is not free to make his own rules in our scientific world. It is never right to argue for 5 ounces in a pound, for spelling pneumonia without a "p," or for making two plus two equal seventeen. There is place for dogmatism in religion where God has spoken. The well-known Presbyterian theologian, Benjamin Breckinridge Warfield, was asked by a lady from Princeton to pray for peace at the coming General Assembly of that denomination, because trouble was anticipated. His response was, "I am praying that if they do not do what is right, there may be a mighty battle."[5]

Those more than ready to give up certain convictions for the advancement of church union, need reminding that anything that is mine I can cede, but what is God's is not in my right to give up. With our private property we can be liberal. With our Lord's written will we ought not tamper. Where in scripture is the church instructed to make her own rules if God's regulations dissatisfy? Rather, where the Lord has spoken, his people do not have the right of veto. The tail is not to wag the dog, but the dog can wag his tail. The church body is to follow the directions from Christ, its head, not the other way around.

A major problem confronts the followers of Christ today. All in the Reformation and Restoration stream of history considered the Bible and the Bible alone as its standard and norm. A doctrine of authoritative revelation in Scripture turned all the adherents to the Bible for answers. In those days belief in the inspiration of the Book of books led to the conclusion that the teaching therein was authoritative. In this day liberal Protestantism seems to be following that segment of Biblical scholarship that is undermining confidence in the Book as revelation. Losing the anchor of infallible Scripture, many self-professed "liberals" are suggesting church traditions as an available hitching post.

There is little doubt that the Bible is either absolute or obsolete. To extend the terminology "Word of God" to include "Tradition" is to relegate Scripture to the category "meaningless," as far as the locus of unity is concerned.

The underlying question, before we take the apathy road to restructuring denominations in organization, faith and practice, is whether or not the Bible is God's Word. If it is, men must conform to its revelation or rebel against it. If it is not, the church's goal should be dissolution rather than oneness. Jesus' question should be answered regarding any religious practice: "from heaven, or from men?" (Matt. 21:25).

Those, whose reliance on Scripture is as firm as ever, have difficulty in a proposed united church where infant baptism replaces believer's baptism. Such an issue has not to do with water, but to Christ's Lordship. On whose terms is entrance into the church to be followed? Are we to go back several centuries to traditions that have developed, or all the way back to the Nazarene who claimed "all authority in heaven and on earth" (Matt. 28:18)? Will we give full leeway to men charting tomorrow's united church, or shall we listen to King Jesus? The wisdom of men or the widom of God offer alternate routes.

When Duke K. McCall accepted the presidency of Southern Baptist Theological Seminary, he affirmed, "It is not the task of a seminary to say what God should have said or what God would say, but simply to chip away the barnacles which accumulate about what God *did* say." Noah built the ark God designed (Gen. 6:15-16). Moses constructed the tabernacle, following the Lord's revealed pattern (Gen. 25:40). Bible "believers" want to build by the revelation left to us and not by the amended versions provided by modern theological carpenters. Christians want their church to look like that modeled in Scripture. The Bible program for unity is a plea for unity in the faith, not for unity of all religious faiths in a restructured denomination.

Listen to J. Robert Nelson:

> Apostolicity inheres primarily in the message of salvation which the apostles knew and proclaimed on the basis of their knowledge of Jesus Christ. The pedigree of preaching is a matter nearer the center of apostolicity than the breeding of bishops. Or, conversely, the distance from the apostles is more readily seen in the anaemic faith and teaching of many contemporary churches than in their well-preserved order and ministry.[6]

THE APPROPRIATE WAY LEADS TO REVELATION

"We speak where the Scripture speaks" is a slogan going back at least to the 9th Century, where a book *The Key of Truth* contains the words. The church across the years has believed that what is Scripturally right is religiously right, but what is wrong has no place in Christianity.

To change the world, the One who changes not sent His Son who "is the same yesterday and today and forever" (Hebrews 13:8). He revealed by his eternal Spirit the "everlasting gospel" (Rev. 14:6, ASV) and entrusted it to His unshakable kingdom for proclamation. Any change in perfection would result in imperfection. The perfect message of Christ's church since New Testament times cannot change.

The presupposition of all interested in restoring the faith and practice of the early church is an authoritative Bible. In the early writings of the modern ecumenical movement, the call was for churches to study the Bible. One only wishes that invitation was still the appeal. Edward John Carnell commends and critiques that movement with his observation, "The ecumenical movement sees the evil in disunity, and for this it must be praised. But it does not see the evil in untruth, and for this it must be criticized."[7]

If that opposition view is true, at the same time among the people there is growing interest in serious Bible study. The quest for God's truth by God's people is a thirst that can not be quenched by the words of mere men. The heart cry is, "To the law and to the testimony!" (Isa. 8:20). The disciple of Jesus wants to "hold firmly to the trustworthy message as it has been taught" (Titus 1:9). He or she strongly desires to "stand firm and hold to the teachings (Paul and his coworkers) passed on . . . by word of mouth or by letter" (II Thess. 2:15). Sample the regular churchgoer and you will find a pair of ears open to learning "The way of God more adequately" (Acts 18:26), but closed to any disinformation that is "contrary to the teaching . . . learned" (Rom. 16:17). "Sound doctrine . . . conforms to the glorious gospel" (I Tim. 1:11) and is the "good deposit that was entrusted to (us) for our 'guarding' with the help of the Holy Spirit" (II Tim. 1:14).

Religious leaders were said by Jesus to be "in error because" they did "not know the Scriptures" (Matt. 22:29). David was convinced that, "the word of the LORD is flawless" (II Sam. 22:31 cp. Prov. 30:5). If Old Testament wisemen knew it wrong to "move an ancient boundary stone set up by your forefathers" (Prov. 22:28), New Testament Christians have sufficient wisdom not to follow the modern religious builder who advocates moving from the solid rock of revelation to shifting existential sands. The unity of Christ's church on the basis of Christ's revealed truth is the road to be chosen by any who call Jesus Lord. Paul's letters call Christ "Savior" seven times, but "Lord" 260 times. Only listening to his will and submitting to that will can bring the divided church together.

The teaching Christ delivered to his church must not be sacrificed. What he did not teach must never be piled on men's shoulders to bear. Wipe the dust from your Bibles, for as Jesus said, "These are the Scriptures that testify about me" (John 5:39). The best way to preach down error is to preach up truth. The depository of saving truth is the Bible. Someone said,

> The Bible . . . the book that is older than our fathers, that is truer than tradition, that is more learned than universities, that is more authoritative than councils, that is more infallible than popes, that is more orthodox than creeds, that is more powerful than ceremonies . . . the omnipotent Word of God."

Bible believers will turn to the Sacred Scriptures for God's will. No "*Science and Health*," no "*Book of Mormon*," and no formulation created by uniting denominations since the first century can replace the "Thus saith the Lord" found in the universally accepted revelation of Holy Scripture. Iron and clay, oil and water, inspired revelation and human tradition do not hold together. The Bible truth of unity calls for unity in Bible truth.

Romanism does not believe the Bible alone road is the route to take, for in that view common people cannot understand the book without the Pope and his bishop explaining its meaning.

Ecumenism seems to hold a similar opinion about "laymen" capability of knowing God's will through Scripture without benefit of "clergy" help in formulating creedal statements and discovering church practices. The apostle Paul held a different view. He would write to "the faithful in Christ Jesus" (Eph. 1:2) and openly avow, "In reading this . . . you will be able to understand my insight into the mystery of Christ" (Eph. 3:4).

Endnotes

1. "Christian Unity," an article in the *Christian Standard* of December 1, 1962, p. 3.

2. *Christianity Today*, October 10, 1910, p. 32.

3. Quoted in the *Pulpit Digest* of November 1958, p. 70.

4. "From Athens to Jerusalem," Journal of the National Association of Deans of Women, June 1951.

5. W. J. Grier, "Benjamin Breckinridge Warfield," The Evangelical Quarterly, April, 1950, p. 121.

6. *Criterion for the Church*, (New York: Abingdon Press, 1962), p. 34.

7. *The Case for Biblical Christianity*, (Grand Rapids, Michigan: William B. Eerdmans Publishing Company, 1969), pp. 27-28.

14

UNITY AND THE PRINCIPLE OF RESTORATION

The Good Shepherd who "guides me in paths of righteousness for his name's sake" (Psa. 23:3), guides all his flock toward unity. The path to that objective leads to the "green pastures" of Truth's primacy and the "quiet waters" of Restoration. Jesus "restores (our) soul," our hopes and our dreams. He leads his church to the recovery of its faith, ordinances and life. He anoints each sheep in his flock "with oil" that will bring restored health in convictions and practices.

The concept of restoration is a viable idea. The shortest road to a biblical ecumenicity would be for each congregation and its members to pattern their teachings and actions after the model revealed in the New Testament. Do not too quickly respond that such an idea will not work. If centuries from now the game of basketball had been totally forgotten and no one lived who had ever played or observed such a game, could that sport be recovered if a book of instructions for the old game was found?

147

Anywhere such an old rule book was obtained, the spirit of basketball could be shared in again at that locale.

If an ancient religious sect had become extinct, or had been so modified that it was hardly recognizable, is its restoration in our time possible? Again the answer is affirmative, if some "religious archaeologists" uncover documents that describe its creed, its rituals, its organization and its laws of entrance and discipline. All that would remain would be for persons to follow the uncovered manual and the old religion would be in the world again. In the same way, if Lutheranism or Calvinism had become extinct over centuries of time, these same entities could live anew. However, no one would adopt either Lutheran or Calvinistic theology until reading about each in some newly uncoverd, descriptive books, or hearing about either from newly commissioned missionaries passing on the distinctive doctrines of such groups.

If restoration of sectarian Christianity can rise from the study of original denominational sources, why should some consider it incredible that the restudy of New Testament documents by a congregation could restore that congregation to New Testament standards? It not only can be done, it has been done again and again in community after community.

EMPHASIZE COMMON AGREEMENTS

The genius of the Restoration Movement, led by such stalwarts as Thomas and Alexander Campbell, pointed sectarian partisans away from the peculiarities that divided them to the common ground wherein unity could be found. The germ of division was the pushing of non-essentials. The genius of harmony can be the preaching of the universals. The call of these reformers was to catholicity. From Thomas Campbell's 1809 *Declaration and Address* onward, the oneness of the church was affirmed in a way not typical in Protestantism. "The Church of Christ on earth is . . . one."

The early church Father, Cyprian, defined the "catholic" as that which is everywhere and at all times acceptable by all Christians. That being true, no unique doctrine of a later time can qualify. Only that gospel and its expression, which goes back to the earliest apostolic period of the church, can be normative for all times. Where denominationalism emphasizes peculiarities, catholicity stresses common ground.

Mormonism is known for its peculiarities in practice, such as polygamy in marriage and baptizing for the dead. Christian Science's distinctives are the unreality of sin and death. Ellen G. White's stress was the observance of the Jewish Sabbath and abstinence from eating pork. The return to New Testament days and ways led to dropping man-made names, creeds, organizations and requirements for membership. The call was back to the Bible, the one book on which to base one's faith; back to a confession that would bind us all together; back to a name all believers could wear.

The universal book of authority is the Bible. The universal, or truly catholic, name is Christian. The one confession of faith every disciple of Christ can affirm without hesitation is that Jesus is the Christ, the Son of the living God. The one baptism that is recognized throughout Christendom is the immersion in water of a penitent believer in the name of Jesus Christ. Other "forms" or other "subjects" have been argued, but the immersion of believers is universally recognized.

We take a giant step toward unity when we wear the name above every name and affirm the creed above every creed. When R. M. Bell was president of Johnson Bible College, a correspondent wrote stating, "We should be willing to give up something in order to become a part of the ecumenical church." Bell's response was an affirmation of restoration as the most direct road to ecumenicity. In the article he listed, with substantiating evidence, seven things he personally had already given up for the sake of unity. They were: 1. His false conception of the church, 2. His denominational doctrines and practices, 3. His denominational baptism, 4. His denominational name, 5. His denominational communion, 6. His denominational plan of salvation and 7. His denominational church government.[1]

MINIMIZE CULTURAL ACCRETIONS

Unity is found in the universally accepted truths and in the unpeculiarities of the "catholic" faith, rather than the peculiarities of conviction and concern that are provincial and not world-wide. What it takes to make a Christian has been known from the first day the gospel was preached. The accretions of time have developed ways to become Methodist-Christians, Presbyterian-Christians or Episcopal-Christians. The evidence is in that it takes more than the Bible to make more than a Christian. Hyphenation follows adding, subtracting or altering the original message.

In the gospel, revealed both in the Gospels and in the apostles' sermons recorded in Acts, we can find our unity. That saving, eternal gospel is our foundation. To confuse cultural practices that ever-change with the Christian gospel that never changes, is to invite contention. Some social characteristics of first century people in far-away places are not of necessity to be copied in our place and time. Temporal and local ways of greeting and dressing are in nature but passing practices. The permanent, fundamental truths of the gospel are the essence in which the church's unity consists. There are elements in a congregation at Corinth, Greece or Laodicea, Asia Minor that we ought not try to duplicate if we would and others that we could not reproduce if we tried.

Isaac Errett, in the first volume, first issue and first page of the then new *Christian Standard*, upheld the gospel as the answer to Christian division. He wrote:

The *truth* of the gospel, to enlighten; the *love* of God in the gospel, to persuade; the *ordinances* of the gospel, as tests of submission to the divine will; the *promises* of the gospel, as the evidence of pardon and acceptance; and the Holy Spirit, in and through all these, accomplishing His work of enlightening, convicting of sin, guiding the penitent soul to pardon, and bearing witness to the obedient believer, of his adoption into the family of God.

The gospel of Christ and not the culture of Palestine is what makes a Christian. It is that gospel which both saves individuals coming out of varied cultures and unites them with each other. Our unity will never be found in papal pronouncements nor in the decisions of church councils. The place to turn for direction is not to historic creeds, but to the unchanging gospel. Creating a new denomination to protest denominations would prove as unsuccessful as to fight a war to protest war. Yet, for every local assembly of believers to renew its pledge of allegiance to Christ's gospel — its facts, promises and terms — is the way to arrive at the goal.

John Wesley, looking back at a road not taken, lamented:

Brethren, I am distressed. I know not what to do. I see what I might have done once. I might have said, peremptorily and expressly, "Here I am: I and my Bible. I will not, I dare not, vary from this Book, either in great things or small. I have no power to dispense with one jot or tittle of what is contained therein. I am determined to be a Bible Christian, not almost, but altogether. Who will meet me on this ground? Join me on this, or not at all.[2]

The path Wesley rued he had not taken, is the road still available for our choosing. The ultimate question is, "Is the principle of restoring the church to the revealed gospel right?"

Our decision to that basic question should not be rejected because one of its advocates sounds boastful or another proponent fails to implement the ideal. The sinfulness and imperfections of man do not invalidate the goal of unity nor the way of restoration as the correct route for its attainment. Alfred Lord Tennyson spoke of the options in his time, of choosing between "bigotry of one hand and flabbiness on the other." We rather to-day can choose in strong conviction that the Bible will be our only guide, and yet do so with the humility that recognizes the choosing of the correct destination is not the same as claiming its perfect attainment.

God promised Israel's restoration with the words, "I will restore David's fallen tent. I will repair its broken places, restore its ruins, and build it as it used to be" (Amos 9:11). Peter knew that Christ "must remain in heaven until the time comes from God to restore everything" (Acts 3:21) in a recovery of the whole universe to its pristine condition. Until that coming day, our interest should be in restoring the lost to a relationship with Christ and restoring the lost unity of the saved in their relationship to each other through the gospel.

The *Millennial Harbinger* advocated:

> Union amongst all the disciples of Jesus in the faith once divinely taught, is supremely to be desired; but union of *sects* is as supremely to be depreciated. . . . If the Christians in all sects could be drawn together, then would the only real, desirable, and permanent union, worthy of the name of the union of Christians, be achieved . . . it appears, the only practicable way to accomplish this desirable object, is to propound the ancient gospel and the ancient order of things in the words and sentences found in the apostolic writing — to abandon all traditions and usages not found in the Record, and to make no human terms of communion.[3]

Endnotes

1. *Blue and White*, Volume XXXII, (Kimberly Heights, Tennessee, March-April, 1960), p. 1,4.

2. *Wesley's 'Sermons'*, Volume II, p. 439.

3. Alexander Campbell, Editor, Volume III, Number 5, (Bethany, Virginia, 1832), p. 195.

15

UNITY AND THE PSALMODY OF BELIEVERS

Nowhere are Christians more united than when they sing their faith. Next Christmas season walk by the various church buildings in your town and notice that the carols they sing are the same. In the Baptist church they are singing "Silent Night, Holy Night" without once remembering the words were written by the Roman Catholic Joseph Mohr and his fellow Catholic Franz Gruber composed the melody. The Pentecostal choir is heard caroling, "Hark! the herald angels sing, 'Glory to the new-born King,' " not cognizant that the Methodist Charles Wesley created that favorite hymn. Down the block in the Presbyterian church house, the congregation is joyfully harmonizing, "It came upon a midnight clear, that glorious song of old." Would they delete the Christmas song from their repertoire, if it were remembered that its author Edmund Hamilton Sears preached for the Unitarians although he believed and preached Jesus' deity? Some attribute "Away in the Manger" to Martin Luther, thinking he wrote it for his little boy Hans. That seems not to keep non-Lutherans from joining in the song. "O Little Town of Bethlehem, How Still We See Thee Lie" rings across the evening sky as street carolers from a variety of denominations sing together, even though the hymn's creator was Phillips Brooks an Episcopalian.

The lesson on unity is obvious. All Christians join in the praise for the hymns are exaltations of Christ. They were not written to promote partisan concepts. The principle, of centering on the universally accepted truths in the promotion of harmony, is shown to be valid. Marc Boegner in an old Abingdon Press book observed that, "Every day, from one end of the earth to the other, the Lord's Prayer is read or prayed in more than 1100 languages by Christians of every denomination." Biblical prayers and non-sectarian hymns manifest how united we all are in praise and prayer. It is not only difficult, but it is also impossible, to worship the heavenly Father and wrangle with an earthly brother simultaneously.

It is conceded that all who make it to heaven will be united there and not separated from one another by barriers of human construction. The voices of believers joined in the songs of worship is one foretaste of heavenly joy. Pliny the younger, in his letter of A.D. 112 to Trajan the governor of Syria, had observed that Christians met "on a stated day and sang songs antiphonally to Christ as God." The stated day was the first day of the week, called the Lord's day in honor of Jesus' resurrection on that day. That resurrection established who Christ was and that he was worthy of worship.

Alexander Campbell's first hymn book was entitled *Psalms, Hymns, and Spiritual Songs*. The name determined how the book would be divided into three parts. The "Psalms" section contained in chronological order songs on the life of Christ from the incarnation, through the ministry and beyond the cross to the following resurrection, ascension, coronation and return. The "Hymns" portion, based on the example of Revelation where Christ receives worship along with the Father, were songs of

154

praise to Jesus. The final section, "Spiritual Songs," were songs about the Scripture, prayer, the church and other religious themes. Here again we see the clear path to unity. Center in Christ. Jesus taught regarding the entire Old Testament in all its parts of "the Law of Moses, the Prophets and the Psalms," that it was "written about (him)" (Luke 24:44). He reasoned with his Jewish contemporaries, "You diligently study the Scripture because you think that by them you possess eternal life. These are the Scriptures that testify about me" (John 5:39).

Is there a congregation where Messianic Psalms are not read in the liturgy? Is there a church where the Gospels are not used in worship? Can a sermon be found in the inspired Acts of Apostles that does not center in Christ? It is time to look at what New Testament scholars have found to be early Christian hymns quoted in the Epistles and Revelation. Following the same pattern, they are songs that center in the Christ of the gospel and the gospel of Christ.

The hymn, which is I Timothy 3:16, covers the full-range of gospel story.

> He appeared in a body, was vindicated by the Spirit, was seen by angels, was preached among the nations, was believed on in the world, was taken up in glory.

There in a nutshell you have the incarnation, crucifixion, resurrection and ascension, plus the story's proclamation and acceptance. That was, and is, something to sing about. All Christians, to be Christians at all, must anchor in this unifying faith.

Philippians 2:6-11 has also been identified as an early hymn quoted by Paul. It reads:

> Who, being in very nature God, did not consider equality with God something to be grasped, but made himself nothing, taking the very nature of a servant, being made in human likeness. And being found in appearance as a man, he humbled himself and became obedient to death — even death on a cross! Therefore

God exalted him to the highest place and gave him the name that is above every name, that at the name of Jesus every knee should bow, in heaven and on earth and under the earth, and every tongue confess that Jesus Christ is Lord, to the glory of God the Father.

What you cannot escape noting is that early church psalmody was Christ exalting and gospel centered. Compare the hymns in Paul's epistles with those of John in his Revelation and the same facts are evident. God is worthy of praise because of his holiness (Rev. 4:8) and creative power (4:11). Jesus receives human adoration for the redemption he purchased with his blood (5:9-10, 12-13). Write music like George Bennard's "The Old Rugged Cross" or John Bowring's "In the Cross of Christ I Glory" and all the redeemed will join in the singing. Compose the lyrics for a song like Isaac Watts' "When I Survey the Wondrous Cross" or like Elizabeth C. Clephane's "Beneath the Cross of Jesus" and only the damned will refuse to sing.

Hymnbooks point the way to unity. The songs of the church win their way into human hearts because they uplift the Lord, glory in the gospel and speak to man's basic needs. Write propaganda to promote a religious party, or produce hymns that push some sect, and the work will never make the hymnal. If one such denominational piece of music slips by the editor, it is certain to be removed by the next edition. It is the praise of Christ that unites his followers.

When the Lamb is praised, "every creature in heaven and on earth and under the earth and on the sea, and all that is in them . . . (sing) 'To him who sits on the throne and to the Lamb be praise and honor and glory and power, for ever and ever!' " At Christ's exaltation living creatures say "Amen," elders fall down in worship and all the saved are drawn together. "I when I am lifted up from the earth, will draw all men to myself" (John 12:32), said Jesus. We who desire unity contribute to the church's oneness in every song, sermon and study that centers on our common Savior.

16

UNITY AND THE PERMISSION OF VARIETY

It is written of God that he "spoke to our forefathers through the prophets at many times and in various ways" (Heb. 1:1). The rich diversity in method of revelation in no way threatened the oneness of the truth the Lord gave to Israel. Does that same Deity permit variety in the human response to His gracious truth? Or would diversity in worship and praise lead to disharmony and pandemonium?

The question that needs the Bible's direction for guidance is, "Can there be diversity without disharmony?" In other words, "Must every local congregation on earth have corporate worship times that appear to have been formed by the same cookie cutter? And must each church's service activities evidence having come from the exact same mold?" F. B. Meyer, in an exposition of I Peter, argues:

Oneness of mind does not demand the monotony of similarity,

157

but unity in variety. Not the oneness of a beanpole, or of a pile of bean-poles; but of the plant which with tendril, leaf, and fruit, rears itself aloft in the summer air. Not the oneness of a brick, or a pile of bricks; but of the house, in which so many different materials and contrivances combine to shelter human life.[1]

God the Creator of our universe gave us a world of rich diversity. Marvel at the variety of the flowers. Walk through the garden and enjoy each different kind of tulip. Experience a rose festival and stand in awe of the endless varieties in the rose family of flowers. Hike a forest trail and count how many differing species of trees you come across. Even each tree reveals definite differences between its limbs and its roots, its cones and its leaves. The multiplicity of animals and birds, fish or fauna, point to a single source. We live in a universe, not a multiverse. Monotheism never demands monotony.

God the Revealer of our Bible used prose and poetry, history and hymns, law and drama, epistle and apocalypse; but the Scripture is a unity. Even the four Gospels, while relating the one gospel by which we are saved, are different in style. An illustration of this is to think of the old pump-organ at grandma's house. Play the same hymn, "The Old Rugged Cross," four times through, but each time have different stops pulled out. The same air is passing through the organ — the same music is being played — but anyone can recognize the different sound each time. In a similar way, the same Holy Spirit, working through different penmen, told the same story of Jesus; yet a discerning ear can tell when the gospel message is recorded by John and when it is from Luke. Diversity in style is there, but unity in message is also present.

God the Planner of the church guides us to diversity, but never leads us to division. Unity in diversity is the message regarding the church in the New Testament. There you find some congregations totally Jewish and others heavily Gentile. Customs varied and languages were different in the world into which the gospel came. Converts with varied personal preferences were made of people from different social backgrounds, ethnic origins and local ways of doing things. The new birth did not eliminate human differences, but it did keep them from being divisive. William Robinson in his book, *The Shattered Cross*, asks us to look at the early disciples, twelve in number. He observes:

> They were made up of a collaborator, an extreme nationalist, one who approximated anarchy, fishermen of the well-to-do owner class and worker class, scientific minded unbeliever, a guileless innocent and a scholar. Here was the embryo of the church and it was typical, too.[2]

Robinson's point was that Christ unified persons with rich personality differences. Their love for the Lord and their trust in the gospel brought unity to people very unlike themselves. Common loyalty to the story of redemption, and common love for the Redeemer, cemented together folk with an infinite variety of backgrounds. The use of differing dress, unlike means of transportation or other dialects is no threat to Christian unity. Wide latitude in ways of service and worship can be tolerated among a family of faith where every member of that family glories in Christ's incarnation, crucifixion and resurrection for his or her salvation. Diversity in customs and observances only adds to the splendor of Jesus' church in Orient and Occident.

Unity and uniformity are not the same. To demand singleness in methods is to deny the right of diversity. When Barnabas and Paul experienced "a sharp disagreement" (Acts 15:30) in missionary strategy, they did decide against traveling together in their next evangelistic thrust. Barnabas teamed up with Mark and Paul with Silas in the service of the Lord, but neither team considered itself in competition with the other and never did one team set out to interfere in the success of the other.

Every congregation of Christ's people in Jerusalem, and in all Judea and Samaria, and to the ends of the earth" (Acts 1:8) became Christians in the same way of accepting the gospel message and being baptized (2:41). These uniformly "devoted themselves to the apostles' teaching and to the fellowship, to the breaking of bread and to prayer" (2:42). Luke's list of these four elements, as the characteristics of Christian worship everywhere from Jerusalem to Rome, were distinguishable marks in each locale. But to this day this oneness in teaching, fellowship, communion and prayer allows for diversity.

THE APOSTLES' TEACHING

The boundaries are set by God. The teaching in "all the churches of Christ" (Rom. 16:16) is to be "the apostle's teaching." No place is left for the doctrines of astrologers, Hindu gurus, Mormon missionaries, New Age mediums, or any other cult representatives. The gospel taught must measure up to that one given by Christ's appointed witnesses.

Within those perimeters diversity is permitted. Should little ones sit with their parents during the Lord's day gathering, or should they be dismissed to another room for "children's church?" Is twenty to thirty minutes the appropriate length for the lesson of the day or would forty-five to fifty minutes be more productive? Can the sermon be brought by an elder, deacon or some other designated person, or ought it always to be delivered by the full-time preacher?

Since "you teach and admonish one another . . . as you sing" (Col. 3:16), can these songs be projected on a screen, or is it best to use a hymn book? Should they be short, repetitive choruses or the old gospel song? Must all the verses be used? Does it become formalism if Scripture is read responsively Sunday by Sunday from the back of the hymn book? And, since visual education is highly recommended by educators, ought preachers be permitted to use object lesson sermons? What about the visual teaching of a baptism? Would it be permitted for a father to baptize his own daughter or a soul-winner to help immerse his or her own convert? Must that be done only by the "local minister?" One Southern California church, facing a parking problem with its "first service, Bible School, second service" order, eliminated the Bible School time — shifting it to mid-week nights. The immediate result was 300 more in attendance each Sunday morning. Was that alteration acceptable?

The permission given every local assembly is to find the way to reach the largest number with the most lasting impact for the gospel. One method working in the Southwest, may not be effective in another place. If "the apostles' teaching" is the subject matter, variety in approach is not only permissible, it is to be commended.

THE FELLOWSHIP

In memory of the resurrection of their Lord, his church met on "the first day of the week" (Acts 20:7). People can only fellowship together if there is a stated time and place. The day has been designated as "the Lord's Day" (Rev. 1:10), but the hour can vary according to the needs of the community. Getting the cows milked and the chores done, before hitching the horses to the wagon for the ride to the gathering place, made eleven o'clock a good morning hour for corporate worship. Today's needs are different and in some places services may begin at seven, eight, nine or whenever. The place may be a hut in Thailand or a church-house in Boston. A bell may toll the hour in Europe or a hollowed out drum beat the assembly call in Africa. The proper attire may be a sari in India, an open-neck shirt in Hawaii or a shirt, tie and suit in Indiana. Variety in dress or in sound, in hour or in meeting place is only beautiful testimony to the world wide nature of God's one church.

"Fellowship" or "partnership in the gospel" (Phil. 1:5) can be a "matter of giving and receiving" (Phil. 4:15). In "the collection for God's people . . . on the first day of every week" (I Cor. 16:1-2), should there be a box by the door or should offering trays be passed to accommodate the people? One congregation may pass the box by the people, another may allow the people to pass by the box.

Here a church decides that serving coffee and donuts, before a class begins its study, might help encourage young adult attendance. There a group prefers no eating in the building where the church assembles. Here a congregation observes special days, like Mother's day or Veteran's day, hoping to bring more people out to hear gospel preaching. There a local body opts to treat every day alike. Such divergence in practice has nothing to do with Christian unity. It is rather an expression of the church's liberty. If Christian oneness meant total conformity in methods, such unity could never exist.

THE BREAKING OF BREAD

The Lord's day without the Lord's Supper, in the church of the early centuries of its existence, would never have been contemplated. They joined in testimony to Christ's crucifixion and resurrection. The gathering at the table of remembrance was one of the givens. Variation in style of communion observance may differ, but everywhere Christ's people come to his table, as he asked.

In one place the reading of the words of institution are always heard. In another, other Bible thought and Bible verses are shared. One congregation I often visit invites the worshipers to come to the table and partake, while many rather pass the emblems to the people. Another group, I occasionally worship with at night in my travels, invites those absent at the morning worship hour, to come to the front for sharing the bread and cup they missed at the daylight service. Still another congregation passes the supper to all at the evening session, seeing no reason to have the morning attenders sing again, pray again, listen again but not commune again. For health reasons, many congregations use individual communion cups, rather than a single cup. For symbolic reasons, some churches prefer that each person "break bread" rather than only pick up a piece of pre-cut bread. Does it really have eternal consequences if the communion conclude the hour together or come prior to the preached message?

The Master's instructions were, "Do this in remembrance of me" (I Cor. 11:25). He did not pass out booklets of detailed instruction to cover every imaginable contingency. He did not require that these itemized rules be duplicated and sent out to every congregation so the ritual would be exactly the same in every kingdom outpost. A variation here or there would not hamper the united witness of the church to God's love, Jesus' sacrifice or the believer's enjoyment of salvation.

THE PRAYERS

As with teaching, fellowship and communing, the prayers will be in every church, even if forms will vary. In one city, where one congregation has the custom of all the church kneeling at the time of prayer, across town another flock meets where here and there some members may be lifting their hands as well as their hearts in the intercession. In one congregation an elder or evangelist may lead the people in a prayer so well-worded, it is evident that the spokesman spent as much time in the careful preparation of his prayers as of his sermons. In the next town the populace seldom heard a prayer that was not *ad lib*.

Some define a "psalm" as a song of praise and a "hymn" as a song or prayer. Both are addressed to God and in that way are different from "spiritual songs" in which we exhort one another. It is considered fitting by most that an entire congregation could join in singing "The Lord's Prayer," or that one voice could vocalize the prayer to which the others could join in the "Amen." In this place the melody may be sung in unison. In that location four part harmony may be heard.

Once again we need to be admonished that uniformity would cramp diversity. But unity is consistent with diversity. Diversity is tolerable among disciples of the Master, when devotion to that Master is unquestioned. "One Lord, one faith, one baptism" (Eph. 4:5) indeed, but not only one way to teach, one college to support or one method of doing mission work. "One body and one Spirit . . . one hope . . . One God" yes, but not only one order of worship, one posture for prayer, or one style of caring for the needy. Let the common gospel unite us. Let God's uncommon love inspire us. Let unity with diversity prevail.

Endnotes

1. *Tried by Fire*, (Springfield, Missouri: Gospel Publishing House).
2. (St. Louis, Missouri: Bethany Press, 1984), p. 42.

17

UNITY AND THE PERVERSION OF FREEDOM

No unity can pass as "the unity of the Spirit" (Eph. 4:3) that does not allow for freedom, because the Bible shouts out the truth, "where the Spirit of the Lord is, there is freedom" (II Cor. 3:17). There is a genuine "freedom we have in Christ Jesus" (Gal. 2:4). We "were called to be free" (Gal. 5:13) and no scheme of union, that calls for forfeiting liberty and becoming "burdened again by a yoke of slavery" (Gal. 5:1), is to be considered the route God would have us travel.

Reach into your pocket and take out a coin. Observe the inscription, "In God We Trust." Note that you are holding a two-sided coin. One coin face speaks of unity. There you will read the words "United States of America." Ponder the Latin phrase *"E Pluribus Unum,"* meaning "the many (are) one." Keep before your mind the truth that this banding together in oneness is the other side of the same coin that calls for freedom. Now let your eyes scan either the quarter, dollar, nickel, dime or penny for its symbol of deliverance from bondage. Do you see the Liberty Bell or Eagle? Can you find the word "Liberty?"

The familiar plea for both unity and liberty join concepts that cannot be separated. Liberty will not long exist where people will not live together in a responsible unity. Unity is the other face of the same coin of freedom. We can neither enjoy unity without liberty nor freedom without unity.

A FREE NATION

The dream of a free church in a free nation burned in the mind of the unity advocate of the eighteen hundreds, Alexander Campbell. He envisioned Christ's prayer for Christian unity being more possible than ever before in a land of liberty. In Campbell's mind, Thomas Jefferson was doing for a nation what his father Thomas Campbell was accomplishing for the church. From the former came the historic document "The Declaration of Independence." From the latter came the historic document the Declaration and Address," the initial step in the Reformation of the Nineteenth Century with its central plea of unity by returning to First Century faith and practice. A scanning of Millennial Harbingers for announced brotherhood gatherings across the years, reveals July 4 as the time constantly selected. The practice continues to this day. The Oregon Christian Convention for over 136 years has assembled the week prior to July 4. The Churches of Christ in the Northwest meet in Tacoma for an evangelistic lectureship each year just prior to, or immediately following, the same date. The people of every nation under the yoke of dictatorial governments long for some future day of liberty, although such a day may never come. Communist rule in Eastern Europe was kept in power for decades only by tanks and guns. The hunger of the human heart for liberty refuses to let slavery have the final say. God's Old Testament Israel tells the sad story of Egyptian bondage, Babylonian captivity and Assyrian subjection; but it also tells the glad story of restoration to freedom. Honoring

God is a key to liberty. Horace Greeley believed, "It is impossible to enslave mentally and socially a Bible-reading people." William Penn declared, "Those people who are not ruled by God will be ruled by tyrants." In a lecture at Harvard Medical School, Erich Fromm, a professor of Psychoanalysis from the University of Mexico, gave this important warning, "We make machines which act like men, and produce men who act like machines. The danger of the 19th century was that we might become slaves; and the danger of the 20th century is not that we become slaves, but that we become robots." Let us cling to the God-given right of humans to think for ourselves.

Americans like mentally to travel back to the Continental Congress and witness John Hancock inscribing his name to the Declaration of Independence. As his name goes down as the first signature in this immortal document, we hear him utter, "I am going to write my name so big and bold that King George can read it without his spectacles."

In more recent times a Bible-school teacher was so proud of her nation and its freedom that she took before her class of little ones a copy of this famous Declaration of Independence. She tried to explain to her tiny tots how important it was and what it meant. Then, holding the document before their excited eyes, she said the simple words: "This means we are free." Immediately a hand shot up in the back of the class and a wee voice disgustingly insisted, "I'm not free. I'm four!" That suggests a question we should always ask. "Am I free?" "Would I be more free, if I followed the unity proposal advocated by this group or that?" Liberty in Christ is never to be sacrificed. To be a free nation in the free world allows for higher freedoms yet.

A FREE CHURCH

The State Church system resulted in persons, born in a certain land, automatically being baptized in infancy into the Roman Catholic Church, the Greek Orthodox Church, or some other national entity. If the New Testament is to be the Christian's guide, such a situation can not be imagined. In Bible days church membership was voluntary. Each convert entered the church by conviction, not by compulsion. Where in Scripture is there a church member that did not want to be? We can affirm correctly that nothing can be considered moral that is not voluntary. A free church entered at will is the only kind of congregation we meet in Apostolic times.

If I would model after God's Word, I will preserve my right of private judgment and the congregation of which I am a part must keep its right to administer its own affairs. As guided by the Scripture, a free church has the inherent right to choose its elders, deacons, preachers and missionaries. Freedom demands voice in the choice of literature helps, agency relations or methods of operation.

Agencies created to offer assistance to churches, such as a college, a missionary group or a publishing establishment, must not be confused with the divine institution of the church itself. The latter is of God's creation. The former, created by Christian people, offer helps where they are wanted but ought not mistake themselves for the eternal. A free church is as free to choose an agency's services as it is to choose not to do so. Unity proposals ought not to mistake a congregation's loyalty to Christ for commitment to work through a particular school, missionary society or printing press.

We are to be free people in Christ. We are free to do as we please in any given circumstance, providing we please to be true to the Lord and to the revealed principles of the Lord's church. A union maintained by burning, bashing or silencing dissenters; or a oneness kept by excommunicating any who will not submit to a bureaucracy; is less to be desired than "the spontaneous cooperation of free people in Christ."[1]

A FREE PEOPLE

Local autonomy is Biblical, and so is personal autonomy. I

cannot hold to the Islamic doctrine of "kismet" or fatalism. I fail to understand Calvin's concept of predestination and eternal security, for while the Bible teaches that God has predestined that the saved will be conformed to image of his Son (Rom. 8:24), I do not see evidence that he has predestined from eternity past which individuals are to be lost. Had he done so, God would be spoiled for us. Then, all the crime and corruption of the world would be ultimately the Creator's fault. Not only would such a doctrine spoil God for us it would spoil us for God. I know the heavenly Father is glad when humans respond to his loving acts with praise. How could Deity rejoice at a prodigal's return, if the sinner were but a robot unable to react other than programmed. To be a puppet responding to pulled strings, is not to be a man. Humans have free will. Free men are free to follow Christ's road to unity.

In 1868 Isaac Errett suggested, "Let the bond of union among the baptized be Christian character in the place of orthodoxy — right doing in the place of exact thinking; and, outside of plain precepts, let all acknowledge the liberty of all.[2] That "liberty of all" must be respected. Reuel Lemmons, in an editorial for the *Firm Foundation*, declared:

> One of the greatest advantages of the Restoration principle is that it allows for intellectual freedom in approaching God's Word. None are forced to strain their religion through the mind of another. None are forced to think within the framework of preconceived religious dogma as outlined by men, however brilliant they may be. Each must be left free to think for himself, limited by God alone. Our patience wears thin with those who are bent on making the brotherhood goosestep.[3]

The liberty to think — freedom belonging to all Christians — implies the responsibility of those interpreting the Bible for themselves to be serious students of the Word, knowing how to use the available tools of concordance and lexicon. Only intelligent use of hermeneutical questions can uncover the original intent of the Biblical books.

Having come one by one into the fellowship of the redeemed by responding affirmatively to the gospel call, we can remain united in that grand fellowship by the continual hearing of Christ's voice and following him alone. Abraham Lincoln's concern was that "no nation can long endure, half slave, half free." My concern is that a congregation's endurance is threatened, when it is half denominational, half free. For if a congregation's sectarian ties will not allow the right of a member to be different, it has forfeited the member's right to be free. Robert Richardson insisted that the unity taught in heaven's revelation is "unity in a person (Christ), with every man having a right to think for himself." The fetter and bonds that go with denominationalism can and ought to be shunned by the believer who can affirm with Paul, "Though I am free and belong to no man, I make myself a slave to everyone, to win as many as possible." (I Cor. 9:19).

Endnotes

1. The definition of Christian unity attributed to Frederick D. Kershner.

2. Quoted in "A Logical Basis for Unity between Churches of Christ and the Disciples of Christ," p. 71.

3. March 23, 1971, p. 178.

18

UNITY AND THE PLUMB-LINE OF APOSTOLICITY

A desire for unity needs a plan for unity to make it practical. The restoration of apostolic Christianity is the surest plan and offers the shortest route to the attainment of Christian unity. The oneness enjoyed in the first century of the church was the result of hearing and heeding Christ's apostles. The same unity can be experienced in our day by following again the teaching of these Christ-chosen men. It is no accident that the earliest baptized believers continued in what Luke called "the apostles' teaching" (Acts 2:42).

The twelve and Paul were directly selected by Christ and were promised miracle power to confirm their teaching. It was made clear that their utterances would be guided by God's Spirit and binding on his church. There is no reason for the church today to search for a basis for unity. Such a basis was revealed long ago. Our mission is to present that basis already revealed in the New Testament Scriptures. In the days of the Apostles, unity was at-

171

tained under their direction. The same oneness can be enjoyed again by returning to the faith and practice that prevailed before division made its inroads.

Since the Holy Spirit has providentially preserved until our day the Lord's words and the words of those who knew him best, we are free to follow that revelation. In every area of life a standard or source of final authority must be found. A dictionary settles how a word ought to be pronounced and what it means. A standard of weights and measures, or a norm for values of currency, make possible the world of banking and commerce. The plumb-line by which to check the church's practices, beliefs and life is not any teaching pre-apostolic or post-apostolic, but apostolic.

THE PRE AND POST APOSTOLIC NORMS

If the question "What time is it?" brought conflicting answers from the masses, we would know how to unify the responses. Each person arguing that he was correct, until one debater convinced the others, is one way. Another option could be compromise. If I believed it was 8 a.m. and you thought it was 8:30, we could each give up a little and settle on 8:15. In the religious world that would mean, if I held for immersion and you contended for sprinkling, a compromise might be made for the use of a bucket of water. Or, if you, under Roman influence, desired a daily mass and another under Jehovah Witness' teaching preferred an annual occasion for the Lord's Supper, perhaps settling on a once a quarter or once a month schedule would be the acceptable compromise. Yet, the disagreeing watches and doctrines can be brought to unity by calling standard time or a standard teaching. Then each party, if willing to admit the need to reset by the standard, could return to the norm. This would not only assure giving the right time or teaching but would contribute to unity.

Where is the standard or norm to be found by the followers of Christ? Might it be in post-apostolic times? Some modern practices, such as "the sinner's prayer" or "the mourner's bench" go back to the revival times on the American frontier. Charles G. Finney in his *Lectures on Revivals of Religion* discusses why the "anxious seat" was being used in the call for decisions to be on the Lord's side. Note his clear recognition of the different instruction being given in the present from that in Biblical times. He wrote:

> The church has always felt it necessary to have something of this kind to answer this very prupose. In the days of the apostles *baptism* answered this purpose. The Gospel was preached to the people, and then all those who were willing to be on the side of Christ were called in to be *baptized*. It held that precise place that the anxious seat does now, as a public manifestation of their determination to be Christian.[1]

When Peter Cartwright asked Raccoon John Smith the significant difference between the mourner's bench and water baptism, he answered, "I'll tell you the difference. One came from the sawmill and the other came from heaven." When will the church learn that the entrance steps given by Spirit-guided apostles are not improved upon by the inventions of later men? Shall we Christians accept creeds or sacraments as normative that do not trace to Jesus? Is that going far enough back? Is not the stream more apt to be purer at the source, rather than down-stream where community after community after community have let pollutants into the stream?

A woman hired a maid to help with the housework. Taking the new employee room to room, the lady of the house was giving careful instruction, especially because of so many antique items. "Be very gentle in cleaning the bedroom furniture," she warned. "It goes back to Louis XIV." The girl responded, "Don't feel bad Madam, my whole kitchen set goes back to Sears the fifteenth." The suggested question is "Are we going back far enough in our search for a norm?" Some pattern their congregations after the revival times of the 1800s, some after the emphasis of reformers in the sixteenth and following centuries, still others after the church councils stemming from the time of Emperor Constantine. Since "the faith was once for all entrusted to the saints" (Jude 3) in Century One, how can accretions of post-apostolic days be demanded of all believers in Jesus?

Another individual or religious group may want to direct us all to pre-apostolic norms. They want us to sing "The Old Time Religion," especially the stanza that says, "It was good enough for Moses and it's good enough for me." No person, aware of the Biblical distinction between the Old and New Covenants, can join in that song. The seventh-day Sabbath, the food laws of Leviticus, the Jerusalem temple and its priesthood with all the rituals and sacrifices relating to it and the holy days, etc. were a part of an old covenant between the Jewish nation and the Lord inaugurated at Mount Sinai. Paul reminds us that God had "canceled the written code, with its regulations . . . nailing it to the cross" and for that reason the Christian was not to "let anyone judge" regarding feasts or fasts, including the "Sabbath day" (Col. 2:14,16). The predicted "new covenant" had been instituted by the Messiah and it was "not . . . like" the first (Heb. 8:8-9). The purpose of the Old Covenant with the Jewish nation was to prepare the world for the New Covenant. The former "was put in charge to lead us to Christ . . . now . . . we are no longer under the supervision of the law" (Gal. 3:24-25). Moses, the old lawgiver and deliverer, served as a type of Jesus, who would deliver his people, not from Egyptian bondage, but from the bondage of sin. All covenants consist of parties, terms and promises. In the old contract the parties were God and physical Israel. The terms were obedience to the law given through Moses and the promises were national blessings. The new covenant is between Christ and the church, the new Israel. We are promised eternal blessings upon obedience to Christ's law.

Jesus did not come to just patch up Judaism, as one would put a new patch on an old garment. His covenant of grace was a

174

new wine that could not be contained in the old wineskin of yesterday (cp. Matt. 9:16-17). The New Covenant church is not to be conformed to the teachings of Moses but to the mind of Christ. The mind of Christ was made known to his apostles and preserved for future generations in the oral and written teachings found in the New Testament. The apostles were given legislative authority for the gospel age. It is the local church elders who have the God-given executive authority to see that the apostles' teaching be carried out in every local congregation, while the church age continues.

THE APOSTOLIC NORMS

To teach the gospel approved by the Lord's apostles is to be on solid ground for ecumenical progress (cp. Gal. 1:6,10). Gene A. Sonnenberg reminds us that "the Bible is not one big Rorshach ink blot form which to read whatever we so desire."[2] The Bible is for our discovering of God's will for us. We say, "Where there is a will, there is a way." We might add, "Where we have God's will, there is God's way." The will of Christ has been made known to us in the apostolic writings. Therefore, in a study of the length and breadth of apostolic teaching, Jesus' way to unity is to be recovered. It is the church envisioned in the mind of the Savior and reflected in the apostolic documents that each congregation should set out to restore.

Please carefully note that it would be of no value to make your congregation resemble the Ephesian church that had "forsaken (its) first love" (Rev. 2:4) or the Laodicean congregation that was but "lukewarm" (Rev. 3:16). It would be equally foolhardy for me to pattern my congregation to the "worldly" traits of the Corinthian believers (I Cor. 3:1). But it would be a blessing to us both to bring our local flocks up to the correct teaching from heaven, written to these people falling short of the ideal. The call for restoration is not a call to old ruts but to the old paths.

It is important, likewise, to see that a return to New Testament faith and life does not mean leaving modern customs for ancient ones, nor wearing strange old styles rather than present-day attire. The teaching of Christ, regarding eternal salvation, ever-needed attitudes or lasting values, are needed in all centuries, whatever the passing fads or fashions.

We will be profited to distinguish, as well, the revelation of the gospel message and its miraculous confirmation. A gift is more important than the wrapping in which it comes. As the apostles "went out and preached everywhere . . . the Lord worked with them and confirmed his word by the signs that accompanied it" (Mark 16:20). Paul called "the things that mark an apostle" as "signs, wonders and miracles" (II Cor. 12:12). The miracles through apostolic hands gave credibility to the new message they were preaching. One miracle — the ability for men of Galilee to speak in whatever language was needed in communicating the wonders of God — convinced thousands of the truth of Christ in Acts 2. One miracle — the instant and total healing of a well-known beggar by the hands of Peter and John — turned many more Jews to accept the credibility of the crucifixion-resurrection story according to Acts 3.

The gospel message, once confirmed in apostolic times, stands confirmed for all time. A miracle written serves the same purpose as a miracle wrought. As the apostolic age drew to a close, the last living witness to Christ's resurrection, recorded "that these are written that you may believe that Jesus is the Christ, the Son of God" (John 20:31). The point being made is that the unity of believers in our day does not demand the restoration of miracle-working. All it requires is the believing, practicing and preaching of that gospel given for all time and confirmed at that time when the message was first told. Some first century wonders like the giving of "prophecies . . . will cease" or the speaking in "tongues . . . will be stilled" (I Cor. 13:8). What will not pass away, but rather abide (KJV) or "remain," will be the Christian "faith, hope and love" (I Cor. 13:13) that all of the apostles revealed.

If I lost my car, the police would be most helped in its recovery by a detailed description of make, model, color, license number and other distinctive features. It would not be essential to be able to trace tire tracks for two thousand miles. Some advocate tracing the "historic episcopate" over the last two thousand years on the theory that only those ordained by the hands of persons in unbroken line from the apostles constitute an authorized "clergy" to carry out Christ's orders. "Apostolic succession," as the doctrine is called, stands on a flimsy foundation. One link missing in the very long chain and the entire theory falls. Why lodge our hopes on a lost map, when the teaching of the apostles is available in the canon of Holy Scripture. To question the years of ministry by thousands of preachers, faithful in teaching the message as given by the apostles, because they have not been ordained by the right (?) hands is bold egotism. Yet, there are those to this hour, who believe unity will only come when today's preachers "accept the office of bishop" and submit to reordination. The question that ought to be asked is not, "Were the right hands on my head?" but "Are the right truths in my heart?"

On this claim to apostolic sucesion, James D. Bales wrote:

If one wants to grow watermelons in California, and there are watermelons in Goergia but not in California, how can one do it? Is it necessary to grow a watermelon vine from Georgia to California in order to do it? Not at all. All that is necessary is to take the watermelon seed and plant it in California and give it the proper conditions of growth. The seed is the important thing.[3]

Arley E. Moore writes:

Lord Davidson, ex-Archbishop of Canterbury, said, "The Roman Catholics want unity, but the condition is that we pass through an arch over which is inscribed, *submission*. . . . Protestants who advocate a loose alliance of religious denominations which they call 'union,' would have us pass through an arch on which are inscribed, *concession, accommodation* and *compromise*."[4]

The arch under which we ought to pass is rather marked *apostolic*. The last apostle to walk on this earth wrote, "We are from God, and whoever knows God listens to us . . . this is how we recognize the Spirit of truth and the spirit of falsehood" (I John 4:6). The ideals of primitive Christianity are in apostolic writings, not in historic church traditions. When the New Testament Scriptures are rightly divided, the Lord's people will not remain wrongly divided. Lesslie Newbigen, the long-time advocate of unity, discovered that "the quest for unity must . . . be regarded not as an enterprise of men aimed at constructing something new, but as a penitent return to that which was originally given but subsequently denied."

The criteria for salvation laid down by the apostles on the first day of the church was to be unchanged "for all whom the Lord our God will call" (Acts 2:39). These Christ-appointed authorities are not to be dethroned. Returning to original ground is to recover common ground. Barton W. Stone taught:

> Jesus did not pray that all who professed to believe in him might be one; because all that profess to believe, have not true, unfeigned faith — the faith of God's elect. To pray that such might be one with obedient believers, is the same as to pray, that light and darkness might be one — that righteousness and unrighteousness might be one — that the children of the bond woman and the children of the free woman might be one. This would be impossible; such a union would be like that of iron and clay — it is not desireable — it is inadmissable by the head of his Church; for all fruitless trees must be cut down — the chaff must be winnowed away. . . . Such unhallowed union has too long disgraced the Church; weakened her energies — obscured her glory, and withered her influence. It is the strong-hold of sectarianism — a bulwark against Christian union — a heavy weight on Zion's wheels — a gnawing worm on their vitals — the bane of Christianity.[5]

Having relearned that the Lord clearly wills our oneness, while the enemy of souls wills our constant dividing, we have sought guidance from the Scripture. That Book has directed us to preserve freedom, variety and catholicity. It has called us to make truth primary and to discover that truth through apostolic eyes. The next movement toward total reconciliation is clearly marked, but it is an admittedly steep ascent. The trail is demanding but the paradise of which we dream is worth the difficult climb.

Endnotes

1. (Oberlin, Ohio: E. J. Goodrich Publ., 1835), p. 254.
2. "Liberating Local Congregations for Recovery of Apostolic Unity in Mission: A Design for a Grass Roots Ecumenicity" (1989 unpublished dissertation, Fuller Theological Seminary), p. 94.
3. *Soils and Seeds of Sectarianism*, (Rosemead, California: The Old Paths Book Club, 1974,) p. 14.
4. A Divided House: *The Cause, Curse, and Cure of Religious Division*, (Privately published, 1981), p. 355.
5. Elder James M. Mathes, *Works of Elder B. W. Stone, Volume I*, (Cincinnati: Moore, Wilstach, Keys and Company, 1859), p. 255.

PART FOUR

THE CHURCH'S DEMANDING
WAY FOR OUR RECONCILIATION

19

UNITY AND THE PROMISE OF TOMORROW

The road to Calvary is uphill all the way. Jesus made plain to those who would follow him that, like him, they too must "take up" a "cross and follow" (Matt. 16:24). The goal of salvation for sinners was to cost Jesus his life. The goal of unity among believers will also only be attained at a price. Our reconciliation with God demanded Golgotha for Jesus, but his adequate motivation of "the joy set before him (enabled him to) endure the cross, scorning its shame" (Heb. 12:2). Our reuniting as the family of God will not come easy in the church, but our motivation to please our Redeemer should keep us moving toward the objective, no matter the sacrifice required. One uplifting factor in the hardest of times is the promise of tomorrow.

The tension between the "already" and the "not yet," runs through the language of Christianity. We can assert without reservation that in Christ we have been saved, and at the same time anticipate the return of Jesus, when he will "bring salvation to those who are waiting for him" (Heb. 9:28). "I am saved" and "I will be saved" are both Biblical affirmations. The first looks to the past at the time of conversion. The latter is a forward look unto the eternal future. When you were immersed in water, as you began your Christian walk, you were pointing all witnesses back to that wonderful time of long ago when Jesus died, was buried and rose again for you. At the very same time, you were predicting that future day when your dead body would be raised and you would rise to meet your returning Lord in the air. The faith that preceded your baptism was the trusting look to the past, when in 30 AD Jesus took your place in death. The hope that flowed from your baptism looked in anticipation to that glad future moment when faith will be replaced by sight and hope will experience fruition. Since the day you shared in the church's initiatory rite, you have often gathered with worshiping saints at the table of the Lord. Once again you glanced back and then forward, as you took the cup "in remembrance" of yesterday and pledged to do so "until he come" and there be no more tomorrows. Paul is right, God "has rescued us from the dominion of darkness and brought us into the kingdom of the Son he loves" (Col. 1:13). The kingdom of Christ is a *present* reality. Peter is right, "You will receive a rich welcome into the eternal kingdom of our Lord and Savior Jesus Christ" (II Pet. 1:11). The kingdom of Christ is a *future* hope. The point I am trying to make is that the same "already — not yet" tension carries over to the unity question.

Our first Christian experience was to be "baptized by one Spirit into one body" (I Cor. 12:13). In the present hour "there is one body and one Spirit" (Eph. 4:4). Yet, at some future day, we will "all reach unity in the faith and in the knowledge of the Son of God" (Eph. 4:13).

UNITY IN THE ETERNAL FUTURE

We are going to be together in heaven. No one denies that.

184

The most ardent Protestant and the most avid Catholic would agree that all those God has promised to save will share eternity together. The most radical sectarian would join the most zealous ecumenist in agreeing that in the next world heaven will not be sectioned off by denominational fences manufactured on earth. All people walking by faith are "longing for a better country" (Heb. 11:16), when human conflicts are over and perfect peace will regin.

Heaven would not be heaven, if the smog of hot debates polluted the skies of Paradise Regained. The traits of those in Perdition consisted of "hatred, discord . . . dissensions (and) factions" (Gal. 5:20). The attributes, that make "the holy city" a holy city, are the qualities that marked the life of Jesus. Read what constitutes "the fruit of the Spirit" in Galatians 5:22-23 and you will hear heaven described. Read the definition of love in I Corinthians 13:4-7 and you will foresee life in the world to come. The time to come, according to God's "will," is to be the time when he will "bring all things in heaven and on earth together under one head, even Christ" (Eph. 1:9-10 cp. 3:5, 9-14; Col. 1:20; Rom. 8:18-21).

The future hope of Ephesians 4:13 is admittedly a dream not fully realized. But, as Harry Kemps in a Good Housekeeping article said, "The poor man is not he who is without a cent, but he who is without a dream." What Christian does not pray regularly, "Your will be done on earth as it is in heaven" (Matt. 6:10)? The fact of our future oneness in heaven should give direction to our present efforts on earth. What will be the situation at the end of time, ought to be appearing in history now. If we are going to be together in tomorrow's world, we ought to be together today. The new age, yet to be consummated, when God will "restore everything, as he promised long ago through his holy prophets" (Acts 3:21), has already been established in Christ. The head of the Church has expressed his desire for those, who will be united eternally in heaven, to be presently united here. Can tomorrow's goal become today's reality?

When a soldier lay dying in agony, the hospital chaplain asked, "What church are you of?" The sick man responded, "The church of Christ." "I mean," came the reply, "of what persuasion are you?" Looking toward heaven with beaming eyes, the answer came, "I am persuaded that neither death, nor life, nor angels, nor principalities, nor powers, nor things present, nor things to come, nor height, nor depth, nor any other creature, shall be able to separate me from the love of God, which is in Christ Jesus." I confess my faith that I am persuaded that, since Christian unity is the church's essence and destiny, such oneness can be and ought to be manifest in time.

UNITY IN THE IMMEDIATE FUTURE

The state of oneness in the future heavenly city must be the present objective in my city on earth. What is, because of human frailty, but partial, halting and inadequate, can move toward wholeness since prayer is our resource. In hell stands "a great chasm . . . fixed" (Luke 16:26) that cannot be bridged. But this is not hell. Prayer is available and God can do the seemingly impossible. Ask. Do what you can now to bring Christians together. Be ready to do more as the Lord opens doors of opportunity in answer to your heart's cry.

A House of Sunshine wall-motto reads, "He builds too low who builds beneath the stars." Don't be discouraged from praying for unity, in that Jesus promised to answer those intercessions which are in his name and according to his will. It is not in the nature of Christ to leave a job unfinished. "Christians Only" have said, "Unity is our business." I know it to be God's business "to bring all things in heaven and on earth together under one head, even Christ" (Eph. 1:10). I have lived to see minds long closed begin to open again. I have witnessed cold and hard hearts begin to warm again from the refreshing breeze sent from heaven, as believers have called on their Lord.

Prayer for unity, coupled with preaching for unity, has transforming power. Mark records miracle after miracle that happened by just a word from Jesus. The "furious squalls" are recorded to have "died down" until there was complete calm, all at the summons of the Christ, "Quiet! Be still!" (Mark 4:37-39). The gospel "is the power of God" (Rom. 1:16). Release the power! Preach unity in Christ, and faith will come "from hearing the message" (Rom. 10:17).

If you see that we have not "already obtained all this" and that Christ's people have not "already been made perfect," your vision is 20/20. We do have a very long way to go. But hear God's word out. That means it is time to "press on" and to do so with the determination found in the words, "one thing I do" (Phil. 3:12-13). "Proclaim peace" (Zech. 9:10) and the people will practice what you preach. Encourage everyone in your congregation to "serve (the LORD) shoulder to shoulder" (Zeph. 3:9) and watch them join ranks. Talk positively of God's divided people being "reunited," with the admonition to "say of your brother, 'my people,' and of your sisters, 'my loved one' " (Hosea 1:11; 2:1). Then marvel at the Lord's power to reconcile those once divided. Read the dramatic story of Ezekiel 37 to your congregation, your class or your family. Let the object lesson of two sticks joined into one stick in the hand, demonstrate God's will for His people to be "one nation." Emphasize, "There will be one king over all of them and they will never again . . . be divided into two" (v. 22).

The distant future's promise of oneness should control our immediate future's possibility of growing closer to one another through prayer and preaching. Let us "give our attention to prayer and the ministry of the word" (Acts 6:4). Atomic power is but a weak example of prayer power and preaching power. The atomic bomb lies dormant until it is detonated by the pressing of a button or the pulling of a switch. Heaven's uniting power awaits but its release in a divided church by the ignition switches marked "prayer" and "preaching." The promise of perfect harmony tomorrow when God has his way, demands that we allow his will to be done in our hearts right now. Speak to Him about oneness to replace division. Speak for him on the same noble theme.

20

UNITY AND THE PRIORITY OF LOVE

The world affirms that love cannot be commanded and that it must be spontaneous for it to be real. The God of heaven, in spite of scholarly objections, orders his people, "Love the LORD your God with all your heart" (Deut. 6:5). Jesus gave the mandate, "My command is this: Love each other as I have loved you" (John 15:12 cp. I John 3:23). In the Christian religion the injunction echoes, "Husbands, love your wives, just as Christ loved the church" (Eph. 5:25), "Follow the way of love" (I Cor. 14:1) and "Love the brotherhood of believers" (I Pet. 2:17).

There is no way to get around the Bible's clear charge. Hard as the demand may seem it is the only way leading to reconciliation. H. Richard Niebuhr is right, "The road to unity is the road to repentance. It demands turning away from all those loyalties to the lesser values of the self, the denomination, and the nation, which deny the inclusiveness of divine love."[1] Repentance is never easy. Loving the unlovely is beyond human achieving.

How can one love a believer who appears to have been weaned on a sour pickle, baptized in vinegar and anointed with battery acid? Admittedly, there is but a minute handful of those wearing Christ's name who fit the above description. However, you may have met some individual or group that comes dangerously close to bearing the above marks. Is not the command to love outside our capability? The Savior who preached, "Love your enemies" (Matt. 5:44), has no intention of lowering the requirements. His plan is rather lifting his followers by his empowering Spirit.

THE DISUNITY CREATED BY THE UNHOLY SPIRIT

The fruit that grows in a life indwelt by the Holy Spirit includes "love . . . peace . . . (and) gentleness" (Gal. 5:22). The opposite outgrowth of "hatred, discord . . . dissentions (and) factions" (Gal. 5:20) develops from the entirely different source of evil. The followers of the lowly Nazarene bear the mark of heavenly descent. Their paternity is visible in the way they talk and walk. Jesus pointed to the evidence of divine sonship when he spoke, "By this all men will know that your are my disciples, if you love one another" (John 13:35).

The truth will out. Christ's followers will be recognized by the seal of Christ in their foreheads (or thinking) and their hands (or actions). Pretending-disciples will be uncovered as fake-believers once their bitter actions speak louder than their professing words. The world often sees the difference more quickly than the children of light. A back issue of the Wall Street Journal ran this conversation:

> "You have a right to be proud of your town," a visitor observed to the hotel clerk. "I was especially impressed with the number of churches. Surely the folks here must love the Lord." "Well," replied the boniface hesitantly, "they may love the Lord, but they sure as hell hate each other."

Christian ears cringe at such a report. We can deny its truth in ninety-nine percent of the cases. Yet we know that a tincture of truth is there in some localities. Our hope is to erase the shame where it exists. I heard of a sarcastic editorial written against an opponent on the pages of a religious publication. When asked what the article was to be titled, this suggestion was given: "Why not call it 'Go to the Devil' by the author of 'Come to Christ'?" It is hard to understand how the famous tract, "Come to Christ," could have come from the same pen.

Debates in words of ice-cold logic, delivered in heated anger, can win converts — but the converts may be won to the cause of hell rather than heaven. We are admonished "to contend for the faith" (Jude 3), not to be contentious about the faith. The latter will drive people away, where Christ's love would draw those persons to himself. A contentious individual only makes larger the mountain that must be removed before unity can be enjoyed. Someone said, "If bees could know it would kill them to sting people, the stinging business would stop." Martin A. Bunsten observed, "He who has a sharp tongue, soon cuts his own throat." In need of our prayers are those sick souls that only seem to be happy when they are unhappy about something. God never intended orthodoxy to be preserved in vinegar.

We laugh at the story about a party game, where the effort was to see who could look the ugliest. The giggles begin when you learn that the lady who won wasn't even playing. Of the religious persons you know is there one that occasionally acts ugly? Alexander Campbell wrote in his *Millennial Harbinger* of January 1836:

> But, as it seems to me, a more unholy spirit appears no where, than in the columns of some of our religious newspapers. I do not wish to name any one, nor do I wish to contend with any one pledged to a party, and to sustain doctrines which unhappily he has made it his interest to maintain, true or false. I have been so disgusted with this unholy and unrighteous spirit, that I do not read, and am resolved not to read, the breathings of any spirit that refuses to let both sides be heard, and that defends divisions among Christians.[2]

191

Solomon manifested his proverbial wisdom in writing, "Hatred stirs up dissension, but love covers all wrongs" (Prov. 10:12). He went further to observe, "Pleasant words are a honeycomb, sweet to the soul and healing to the bones" (Prov. 16:24). The one wiser than Solomon asked, "If you love those who love you, what reward will you get? . . . What are you doing more than others?" (Matt. 5:46-47). It was Jesus' teaching that "the greatest commandment in the Law (was) love" (Matt. 22:36-39; Mark 12:28-33). The lever that can move the lost toward Christ and the separated believers toward each other is love. Bigotry, or animosity, or intolerance, repels. "Christ's love compels" (II Cor. 5:14). "Love builds up" (I Cor. 8:1).

THE UNITY CREATED BY THE HOLY SPIRIT

Let the modern psychologist note, that the love commanded of Jesus' followers is not sentimental. It is not a vague nice feeling for everyone and everything. Erotic attraction, and friendly amiability toward all, could not be commanded. Emotional impulses don't come as response to orders. The love the believer is to have is described in I Corinthians 13. That ἀγάπη love is "patient . . . (and) kind" (v. 4), revealing the fruit of "Peace, patience (and) kindness" (Gal. 5:22). Such fruit only can develop by the Holy Spirit's residency in the heart. That is what the apostles affirmed in the teaching that "God has poured out his love into our hearts by the Holy Spirit, whom he has given us" (Rom. 5:5).

Fredrick Kershner of Butler University defined Godly love as "intelligent good will." Paul Tillich called love the "drive toward the reunion of that which is separated." These descriptions reveal love as the actions of a person's will, not his or her emotions. Taking "a genuine interest in (another's) welfare" (Phil. 2:20) is another name for love. A brother in the church may hold a distasteful view or harbor a divisive attitude. It would be impossible to feel good about what you see. Nevertheless, it is required that you and I be genuinely concerned about him and anxious for the opportunity to minister to him. Not to sense a responsibility for, and interest in, such a person is not to have the mind of Christ that seeks to build relationships. Without the desire in Christians to get together, Christian unity would be a lamp-wick with no oil source.

The request of the aging John to his church was, "I ask that we love one another . . . that we walk in obedience" (II John 5-6). It is disobedience to fail to love. To love "with actions and truth . . . is how we know we belong to the truth" (I John 3:18-19). To fail the love-test puts one in a precarious position. "If anyone says, 'I love God,' yet hates his brother, he is a liar. . . . Whoever loves God must also love his brother" (I John 4:20-21). Let the most orthodox among us remember, "Everyone who loves has been born of God" (I John 4:7-8). Your baptismal certificate, or your diploma from a "true" Bible College, will not change the above verdict.

The Lord does not withhold his grace from the congregation that falls short of perfection in holiness or doctrine. If you have read I Corinthians you see that God's love is greater than our failures. No higher barrier to unity exists than the notion that God extends his love only to those who have every doctrine straight. View everything in the light of Jesus' compassion that, for so long, bore with the disciples, in spite of their foolish outbursts and slowness to learn.

The West coast evangelist, Elery Parish, tells of attending a Pentecostal gathering in which many were asking for some gift, such as healing, the gift of tongues or the baptism of the Holy Spirit. One voice was heard to plead, "Baptize us in your love so we can get along with each other." Let all the people say, "Amen!" to that needed prayer. Run all your doctrinal trains of thought through the Grand Central Station of I Corinthians 13.

Unity in truth does not ask anyone to go contrary to convictions nor to violate conscience. It does require that the full truth include God's command of love. Love is the engine that empowers the train to follow the track of truth on which it runs. Yes, baptism is a command not to be omitted. So is the order, "love each other deeply" (I Pet. 4:8). Yes, there was a past, when we were "being hated and hating one another" (Titus 3:3). Now there is a present, when we are under orders to "pursue . . . love" (I Tim. 6:11), to "serve one another in love" (Gal. 5:13) and to "live a life of love" (Eph. 5:2). Yes, patterning your congregation after the church revealed in the New Testament has everything to commend it. Nothing is more Scriptural than measuring your personal life after that of Jesus, whose every act revealed his Father's love for all.

Love is the master-key to open doors in the pursuit of unity. No matter how rusty the hinges on which the doors of inter-congregational fellowship swings — no matter how difficult it would be to unlock the sectarian mind — love is able. You see the promise of Spring, after bitter cold-periods of isolation from each other. You can measure a reduction in the sectarian bitterness that once blurred the image of Christ in his church. Gone, or going, are the not-so-good old days when the denomination down the block was painted as being composed of villains or imbeciles. Soon to come, or almost here, are the better times when humility makes us aware that there is blame enough to go around for the church's short-comings.

In the face of differences, anybody can go the separation and divorce route. It takes character to stay together, determined to work out the differences. Commitment to Christ calls for churches and homes to be "rooted and established in love" (Eph. 3:17). Pray, "May the Lord make your love increase and overflow for each other and for everyone else" (I Thess. 3:12). When you already can assert, "You do love all the brothers," you are urged "to do so more and more" (I Thess. 4:10 cp. II Thess. 1:3). "Set an example for the believers . . . in love" (I Tim. 4:12).

In the popular chorus of today, "We are one in the Spirit, we are one in the Lord," there is the line, "And we pray that our uni-

194

ty may one day be restored."[3] Paul wrote, "And this is my prayer: that your love may abound more and more in knowledge and depth of insight" (Phil. 1:9). Love can bring that restoration. Place a lettuce leaf under the hot water faucet and watch it shrivel and shrink. Turn on, instead, the cold water and life appears to come back. Words of anger wilt friendships. Words of love restore life. Let the words of your mouth bring life. Keep the boiling water turned off. To "greet one another with a holy kiss" (Rom. 16:16) will do more for unity than a sermon on the errors of the denominations. A sharp three-inch tongue can slay a six-foot tall opponent, but as Pythagoras observed long ago, "A wound from the tongue is worse than a wound from a sword, for the latter affects only the body, but the former, the spirit."

Be aware how often, in the Bible, you will read, "My purpose is that they may be encouraged in heart and united in love" (Col. 2:2) or "The goal of this command is love" (I Tim. 1:5). Without the ingredient of love, unity can not exist. With love all virtues can be bound "together in perfect unity" (Col. 3:14). That being true, the church's demanding way for reconciliation requires that our "love must be sincere" and that we "be devoted to one another in brotherly love" (Rom. 12:9-10), for we are here "for building you up rather than pulling you down" (II Cor. 10:8). Let your ever outstanding debt be "the continuing debt to love one another" (Rom. 13:8). Pay your debt!

Endnotes

1. Quoted in Ralph Louis Woods, Editor: *The World Treasury of Religious Quotations*, (New York: Hawthorne Books, 1966), p. 1017.
2. Pp.4-5.
3. Copyright 1966, 1967 by F. E. L. Church Publications, Limited.

21

UNITY AND THE PLEA OF HUMILITY

"If" is one of the biggest words in the Bible. Hear a promise from God that begins with that word. "If my people, who are called by my name, will humble themselves . . . I . . . will heal their land" (II Chron. 7:14). Change only the word "land" to "church" and you discover an essential to healing the divisions in the church. Humility precedes the healing. Without it, there can be no restoration of the desired oneness. Unity comes by following the demanding way.

You can not reach the "one body . . . one Spirit . . . one hope . . . one Lord, one faith, one baptism; one God" of verses 4-6 of Ephesians 4, if you by-pass the preceding verses 1-3. The glorious unities named by Paul are the end of a road, beginning with, "be completely humble and gentle; be patient, bearing with one another in love." To be completely humble, in the eyes of the world, was a vice. In the teaching of Jesus, it became a virtue. Ταπεινοφροσύνη means humility or lowliness. That trait became an irreplaceable part of Christian character (cp. Acts 20:19). Πραΰτης, indicating gentleness or meekness, calls for submissiveness in personal relations, as we "gently instruct" (II Tim. 2:25). Μακροθυμία is patience or longsuffering and calls for slowness in avenging wrong, as forbearance requires that we not allow another's faults to keep us from loving them.

The Christian greeting "grace and peace" (I Cor. 1:3) joins words that belong together and must be in that order. Peace can only enter, when grace precedes it. Christian unity — peace within the church — demands the prerequisite of grace in the heart. The attitude produces the actuality.

Learn that God's way up is down. Our platitudes count for little. Our attitudes count for much. F. B. Meyer observed:

> I used to think that God's gifts were on shelves one above the other; and that the taller we grow in Christian character, the easier we should reach them. I find now that God's gifts are as shelves one beneath the other, and that it is not a question of growing taller, but of stooping lower, and that we have to go down, always down to get His best gifts.

Paul spoke of himself as "the least of the apostles" (I Cor. 15:9) in 55 A.D., as "less than the least of all God's people" (Eph. 3:8) in 61 A.D. and as "sinners — of whom I am worst" (I Tim. 1:15) in 64 A.D. Humility to the apostle was the lowest gear that enabled him to climb the steepest hill. It is the only gear that will enable the divided church to reach the heights of oneness. James knew what "causes fights and quarrels" (James 4:1) and he knew the solution to be, "Humble yourselves before the Lord, and he will lift you up" (James 4:10).

OUR ATTITUDE TO GROUPS

The difference between coaching and criticizing is one of attitude. James Burton Coffman states, "A Christian who is always

198

'up tight' about the mistakes of others can create a disaster in any congregation. He, in fact, *is* a disaster!"[1] Did God equip us with two eyes, two ears and only one mouth so we would observe and listen more than we speak? Beating our own breasts for our own shortcomings is preferable to beating the other fellow's head for his failures. You and I may be advocating the truth as it is found in the New Testament; but, until we are achieving it fully, there is room for humility.

"Clothe yourself with . . . humility . . . Bear with each other" (Colossians 3:12-13) and "Let us not become conceited" (Gal. 5:26; Rom. 12:16) are admonitions we need to heed. When our years of careful study have led us to feel certain of our doctrinal conclusions, we need the more to hear God's Book advise, "Do not think of yourself more highly than you ought" (Rom. 12:3). We also need to see that truth from the other side. We should not think of a brother, tied to a denominational system, more lowly than we should. Was it our incredibly good fortune to fall into contact with Christ through a group that used good hermeneutical principles? Was it the other's bad luck to learn of Jesus from a believer who belonged to a group with a point here and there of incorrect exegesis? A rebel against God's will is always anathema. But a servant of Christ with a mistaken view on some side-issue is a brother, in spite of his need for further teaching. It will not be by coercion but by tolerant discussion the problem will be solved and unity attained.

"Be peaceable and considerate, and . . . show true humility to all men" (Titus 3:2) is wise counsel. "Be patient with everyone" (I Thess. 5:14) is good advice for every minister of truth, for a "man of knowledge uses words with restraint, and a man of understanding is even-tempered" (Prov. 17:27). Jesus correctly labeled "arrogance" an evil (Mark 7:22). He, who never compromised the truth of heaven, was a model of meekness. Paul would appeal to the Corinthians, "by the meekness and gentleness of Christ" (I Cor. 10:1) and to the Philippians to have the same "attitude . . . as that of Christ" (Phil. 2:2). The command of the Head of the church is, "in humility consider others better than yourselves" (Phil. 2:3). The prohibition is not to be "boastful, proud, abusive . . . (or) conceited" (II Tim. 3:2,4). That means that "you, man of God" are to "pursue . . . gentleness" (I Tim. 6:11). In the world Christ has turned upside-down, to be "peace-loving, considerate, (and) submissive" is to make you "peacemakers who sow in peace" (James 3:17-18).

E. Stanley Jones analyzes the Pharisee group as advocating salvation by isolation. They were "the embodiment of the Moral Order which pronounced judgment on men." Jones tells of his Chinese interpreter, troubled by the word "Pharisee," asking, "What sea was that?" The missionary thought he should say, "The Dead Sea," for negative attitudes produce only dead results.

Conceit is a barrier to unity. Clovis Chappell, preaching on Jesus' parable of the Pharisee and the Publican, spoke of the Pharisee having a good-eye on himself, a bad-eye on his fellowman and no-eye on God. Being an expert at finding fault is not one of the requirements for being a disciple of the Master. Disciples must be teachable. Friction is reduced to a fraction, when seeking advice replaces only giving advice. It is said that one does not get indigestion from swallowing one's pride occasionally.

In teaching some Apollos "the way of God more adequately" (Acts 18:26), some young Timothy is not to "rebuke . . . harshly, but exhort . . . as if he were (his) father" (I Tim. 5:1). It is never the proper approach to be "overbearing" (Titus 1:7). It is always wise not "to quarrel" but "be kind to everyone" and "gently instruct" (II Tim. 2:24-25). Hear the counsel again: "Deal gently with those who are ignorant and are going astray" (Heb. 5:2). Memorize your job-description: "Be patient and stand firm. . . . Don't grumble against each other" (James 5:8-9). Never forget you are to "be prepared to give an answer to everyone who asks you to give the reason for the hope that you have. But do this with gentleness and respect" (I Pet. 3:15). "Let your conversation be always seasoned with salt" (Col. 4:6).

OUR ATTITUDE TO INDIVIDUALS

It may be well-and-good to humbly teach an erring denominationalist, but what about some "Diotrephes, who loves to be first" (III John)? Divisions in congregations are more often over personal loyalties than doctrinal differences. Alexander Campbell argued, "The pope's chair is found in almost every sect . . . and half or three fourth of all our religion controversies is (sic) about who shall sit in the Pope's chair."

The easiest Diotrephes to eliminate for the sake of unity may be the one hiding in one's own breast. In every church the preacher, or an elder, may allow the power that goes with the position to turn him from a servant of Christ to a manipulator of men. A. T. Robertson in his *Word Pictures* tells of writing an article forty years before on Diotrephes for a denominational paper. The editor reported to him that twenty-five deacons dropped the paper in resentment, feeling the article was written against them. At least the Holy Spirit caused them to see themselves. Authority, unchecked by one's conscience, can corrupt, but does not need to. Just remember that in the word "humility," the "u" comes before the "i." Check your Bible Concordance and note that the word "others" is used five hundred twenty-two times in the Scripture. Jesus healed others, sat at meat with others and saved others. It is time to consider the Platinum Rule of Stetson University: "Think about others as you would have them think about you."

On your part, "Honor one another above yourselves" (Rom. 12:10). As for you, "Watch out for the yeast of the Pharisees" (Mark 8:15). When "in your hearts (you) do not think evil of each other" (Zech. 7:10), there is one less embryo Diotrephes to deal with. When the disciples of Jesus will "submit to one another out of reverence for Christ" (Eph. 5:21), a church split can not happen. J. H. Jowett pointed out, "Don't let us think we need to be 'stars' in order to shine. It was by the ministry of a candle that the woman recovered the lost piece of silver."

Humility can come to those who give a moment of thought to the limitless universe God has created. How meager is every person's knowledge. Someone added, "They that truly know God will be humble; they that truly know themselves cannot be proud." There is little the apostle John could do to muzzle Diotrephes in his day, and there is not much we can do to displace one of his kind that may appear today. But we can determine to model our lives after the Rabbi from Nazareth rather than the rabble-rouser from Ephesus. When we wash our brother's feet, let us refuse to do it in scalding water. When we write up our ministries, let us capitalize the "You," as in many foreign lands, and not capitalize the "I," as is done in the English language. Doubly "blessed are the meek, for they will inherit the earth" (Matt. 5:5), and greatly help unify the church. With Paul tell your fellow churchmen, "we were gentle among you, like a mother caring for her little children" (I Thess. 2:7). Those taught by the Scriptures know that "humility comes from wisdom" (James 3:13). "Do not exasperate your children" (Eph. 6:4), nor your congregation, nor your religious neighbors. "Be made new in the attitude of your minds" and "get rid of all bitterness" (Eph. 4:23, 31), then your service for God will triple in effect. "A gentle tongue can break a bone" (Prov. 25:15).

Learn from the scholar Johann Adam Mohler:

> A choir is constituted when the voices of different persons, men and women, boys and girls, each singing in its own way, are blended into harmony. Without the multitude and variety of the voices, we would have only a tiresome and crippling monotony, and without their blending, only a painful dissonance. The art of the choir master, who must have a keen sense of harmony in order to be able to train others, enables him to recognize the

discordant voice, but his wisdom prompts him to correct that voice, so as to be able to keep it as a constituent part of the choir. When encouraged by the choir master, he who sings the bass must not be led to imagine that because his specialty is the strong, deep note, the lower he sings the better, but he must strive to put the depth and power of his voice in harmony with the sweetness and gentleness of the others. If, unable to notice by himself the dissonance of his voice, he were to take no account of the conductor who is in charge of the performance as a whole, or still worse, if he imagined that he alone could produce the entire melody, he would have to be excluded as incapable of being trained and as hindering the common achievement. He would represent no longer a contrast, since true contrasts are compatable with unity, but would rather constitute a contradiction.[2]

Mohler has given a clear insight as to what every preacher or elder ought to bring to the congregation in which he serves. Choirmaster is an interesting way to look at one's mission. For, bringing each life into harmony with the others, is the leader's task. No *ad libbing* by the players, but carefully following the revealed manuscript with the guidance of the leader, brings out a harmony that makes angels want to join in the song.

Endnotes

1. *Commentary on Galatians, Ephesians, Philippians, Colossians,* (Austin, Texas: Firm Foundation Publishing House, 1977), p. 197.
2. *Die Einheit in der Kirche,* (Cologne: J. Hegner, 1957), Section 46, pp. 152-153.

22

UNITY AND THE PENITENCE OF CHRISTIANS

To win the race against division in the ranks, the hardest hurdle to clear is that of repentance. To call for penitence is ego-smashing. It demands a person admit to sharing in sin. To tell a proud, highly-respected Rabbi, "You should not be surprised at me saying, 'You must be born again' " (John 3:7), seems as insulting as to tell a church-attending Christian "You must repent of your denominationalism." Some writer in an old issue of *Christianity Today* confessed, "Baptists are ready to do *everything else but repent*. They will go to conferences, cooperate and cooperate, tithe their income and adopt programs, but repentance is something else." Exchange the name "Baptist" in that confession to any other of the denominational titles extant and the description will fit.

Only when our party loyalties, that run in our family's tradition for uncountable years, can be sublimated to Christ's will for oneness, will Christian unity have a chance of success. Many believers are finding their love for Christ greater than human ties. Ian Maclaren admitted, "The division of the church into sects is a distinct and flagrant sin." The Methodist, Doremus A. Hayes, wrote, "Division is not to be excused, it is only to be repented, and bewailed, and denounced, and abhorred."

Will family-ties to Wesleyanism, or Lutheranism, or Roman Catholicism prove stronger than our ties to Christ? The question of Jesus is, "Do you truly love me more than these?" (John 21:15). Christ wills the unity of his people. There can come no harmony without repentance, for unity requires the end of all denominations and the surrender of all human names. We rise by the things we put under our feet. Party names, sectarian systems and denominational structures placed under our feet will take us together upward and forward as Christ's one church.

REPENT OF DENOMINATIONALISM

It is Christian to bow our heads in prayer for unity. It is true to Jesus' will to bow our heads in shame for any part we may have had in the continuance of schism. We have long affirmed, "Where the Scriptures speak, we speak." The time has come to avow, "Where the Scriptures speak, we are ready to act." The first act needed is that of repentance.

Alcoholism and division are maladies that can be cured, but recovery can never begin until there is recognition that there is need for a change. The alcoholic delays his or her recovery by refusing to admit to being in a dreadful condition. Human pride holds out to the end. When Jesus spoke of the "poor in spirit," "those who mourn" and "those who hunger and thirst for righteousness" (Matt. 5:3-6), he was describing an essential attitude prerequisite to being "blessed" by a Savior. Those persons shouting, "I am rich; I have acquired wealth and do not need a thing" (Rev. 3:17), are not looking for the offered salvation, as do those who feel "poor" in the spiritual realm. How ready for promised forgiveness is the guilt-ridden soul, who can "mourn" over sins committed against a loving God's will. No man stuffed with pride will "hunger and thirst" for another way.

It is evident that the beatitude or blessing of unity can only be poured out on the church after it recognizes its sinful state in division and longs for "the unity of the Spirit through the bond of peace" (Eph. 4:3). When alien sinners were "cut to the heart and cried out "What shall we do?," the answer that brought salvation was readily available (Acts 2:37). When Christ's people are convicted by the Spirit that sectariansim is sin and call out "What shall we do?," the answer that brings oneness will be forthcoming. The very recognition that our separation is sin and the desire to turn from division to oneness is the beginning of the cure.

It is time to "grieve over the ruin of Joseph" (Amos 6:6). The day has come that we must realize that when "your brother has something against you," you must "first go and be reconciled to your brother; then come and offer your gift" (Matt. 5:23-24), for worship is only acceptable when coming from people living in harmony. The hour had arrived when we, who divide Christ's church like Roman soldiers divided Jesus' clothes, cannot be covered by the prayer, "Father, forgive them, for they do not know what they are doing" (Luke 23:34). We ought by now to know what we are doing. For almost two thousand years, we have had the revelation in New Covenant Scriptures that condemns schism and calls for unity. Ignorance of God's will can not be excused in a people, speaking of themselves as a Bible people.

REPENT OF JUDGMENTALISM

No one is in greater need of repentance than that person who boasts, "God, I thank you that I am not like other men" (Luke 18:11). A splinter group, identifying itself as a "loyal church," or a "faithful people," needs to pray that, when their Master comes seeking for fruit, he not find "nothing except leaves" (Matt.

21:19 cp. Mark 11:13). Those in the Restoration movement, which is working for the unity of all believers, need to recognize that knowing the goal and attaining the goal are not the same. It is wholesome to remember that centuries of creedalism will not be erased overnight. It is good to see that doctrinal loyalty, while a necessity, is not by itself a sufficiency. You, who plead for the observance of the Lord's Supper every Lord's Day, are all your members present at each Sunday assembly? You, who teach a baptism by burial in water to arise to walk in newness of life, do you see that new life in each member? You, who want to be known as "Christians only," does the world see Christ in you?

While doctrinal correctness is a proper goal, and nothing short of that should be a satisfactory aim for any congregation, the danger of being judgmental of others is a trap to be avoided. Jesus warned, "Do not judge, or you too will be judged" (Matt. 7:1). Some people make it a habit to be censorious, biting at others in unjust criticism. Paul wrote of the danger. He said, "If you keep on biting and devouring each other, watch out or you will be destroyed by each other" (Gal. 5:15). Cannibalism, or man-eating, with the teeth is paganism for sure. But devouring another's character with the tongue is equally heathen, even when practiced in a church. A man can be lynched with a label as well as by a rope.

Listen to the preachers, teachers and members in your congregation. Do any of them talk like they were born in the objective case, seemingly always objecting to something? Someone said, "You have to be little to belittle." Another wrote, "Mansions in the sky cannot be built out of the mud thrown at others." The philosopher, Seneca, taught, "It is the practice of the multitude to bark at eminent men, as little dogs do at strangers." The Bible admonishes, "Get rid of all bitterness . . . and slander" (Eph. 4:31). That is as much a Scriptural command as, "You must be born again" (John 3:7).

It is reported that during the Peninsular War, an officer of artillery had just fired a gun with admirable precision against a body of men posted in a woods to his left. The Duke rode up and said in his cool way, "Well, aimed, Captain. But no more. They are our own 39th!" Christian weapons must be directed against our enemy Satan and not misdirected against believers in our common Lord. Think often on "the riches of (God's) kindness, tolerance and patience," for that "leads you toward repentance" (Rom. 2:4). "Brothers, stop thinking like children" (I Cor. 14:20). Fenelon showed maturity, when he reached the sage conclusion, "We can often do more for other men by correcting our own faults than by trying to correct theirs."

Ask why vultures and hummingbirds find different things, as they fly across the landscape. The answer is obvious. They are looking for different things. Buzzards seek and find carrion — dead and putrifying flesh. Hummingbirds seek and find sweetness. You, too, will find fault, if that is what you are looking for. It is time for private prayer: "Search me, O God, and know my heart; test me and know my thoughts. See if there is any offensive way in me" (Psa. 139:23-24). It is time for collective confession: "Confess your sins to each other and pray for each other so that you may be healed" (James 5:16). Once the member of a body of believers is healed of animosity, the whole body will be restored to harmony. The brother with a constant chip on his shoulder should recognize that this attitude reveals there is wood higher up.

"Repent" is the divine command relayed to the sinners in the world. "Repent" is the Lord's injunction to every church with "an ear . . . (to) hear what the Spirit says to the churches" (Rev. 2:7). The Ephesian Church was called on to "Repent" (Revelation 2:5). So were the congregations at Pergamus (2:16), Thyatira (2:21), Sardis (3:3) and Laodicea (3:19). Repentance is the change of mind that leads to a change of conduct. As Dwight L. Moody said, it is in your will, not your handkerchief. God is calling on his church to make a change and keep the change. Sin is not to be explained away, or renamed with a less-offensive title. Sin is to be recognized for what it is. Sin is to be repented of. Sin is to be left behind. After hearing the Lord's prayer for unity in John 17:20-21 and Paul's plea for unity in I Corinthians 1:10-13, you know that living in oneness is good. "Anyone, then, who knows the good he ought to do and doesn't do it, sins" (James 4:17) Repent! For the sake of a lost and confused world needing the only Savior, "Repent!" It is not easy. Jesus' cross was not easy. His love for the lost sheep and the prodigal sons of earth led him to Calvary. Allow his love in each of us to lead us to unity.

23

UNITY AND THE PRESENCE OF GOD

Aristotle knew, "You don't have a man when you have a statue." You know that a coerced union on Christ's body needs the breath of life and not only the outer appearance of structured oneness. "As the body without the spirit is dead" (James 2:26), all union plans without God's Spirit will prove futile. The ancient words of Jehovah, recorded by Israel's prophet, are true as ever: "Not by might nor by power, but by my Spirit," says the LORD Almighty (Zech. 4:6). All who were "saved through the sanctifying work of the Spirit" (II Thess. 2:13) and "baptized by one Spirit into one body" (I Cor. 12:13) are meant to enjoy "the fellowship of the Holy Spirit" (II Cor. 13:14).

The desired unity depends upon our returning not only to the pattern, but to our infilling with the Spirit of our Pattern-maker. We desperately need both the Holy Spirit's blueprint before us and his holy imprint within us. It should not be considered unreasonable that "the unity of the Spirit" (Eph. 4:3), require our openness to the Spirit.

The realization of reconciliation with one another has demands. To name love, humility or penitence, as essential ingredients, is to list qualities requiring God working within his people. If Christian unity is the gift of God, and if his Spirit creates the harmony, does this not relieve us from striving to attain it? The certain answer rings out, "Make every effort to keep the unity of the Spirit through the bond of peace" (Eph. 4:3). The Holy Spirit of God comes into lives and situations where he is invited. He, like the incarnate Son, says to struggling and divided congregations, "Here I am! I stand at the door and knock. If anyone hears my voice and opens the door, I will come in" (Rev. 3:20).

When we realize the failures of our human efforts and recognize our need for heaven's available power, that transforming, life-altering power is ours for the asking. When a Northern river freezes solid in the cold of winter, hundreds of humans with small ice-picks in hand would but fail in their energy-exhausting effort to make the waters navigable. But wait a while until the sun begins to shine and the warm breezes begin to blow from the South, then in short time boats are freed to sail again toward the destination of their choosing.

UNITY WILL COME TO THE "CHARISMATIC" CONGREGATION

Do not be afraid of the term "charismatic." The Greek word Χάρισμα refers to a gift, making a "charismatic" one who has received God's gift. The word, properly defined, refers, then, to every Christian on earth. When you were baptized as a believer you received "the gift (Δῶρον) of the Holy Spirit" (Acts 2:38). Apostles spoke of "the Holy Spirit, whom God has given to those who obey him" (Acts 5:32). It is a divisive error to think that some believers have the Spirit and others do not. The text of Romans 8:9 can not be erased from God's Bible: "If anyone does not have the Spirit of Christ, he does not belong to Christ." We are either

212

in Christ or out of Christ, redeemed or not redeemed, Spirit indwelt or not Spirit indwelt.

The "unity of the Spirit" can be enjoyed only by those in whom the Spirit lives. The more he is allowed to have sway, the closer each believer will come to the other. The Spirit's infilling causes the fruit to grow in the lives of Christ's followers and to be manifest in their thoughts and actions (Gal. 5:22). God keeps his promise, "I will give them singleness of heart and action" (Jer. 32:39). Often Paul's letters begin with reminders that "grace and peace . . . (come) from God" (Gal. 1:3 cp. II Cor. 1:2), so those who desire unity know to whom they must turn. If you and I hope for oneness in the church body, it should be evident "we both have access to the Father by one Spirit" (Eph. 2:18). Jew or Gentile, fisherman or centurion, receive the "same gift" (Acts 11:17). That God has accepted these, he "showed . . . by giving the Holy Spirit to them" (Acts 15:8).

A little girl began to stir with her spoon the cup of tea her mother had served her. After stirring and sipping, then stirring and sipping some more, she complained, "Mother, it won't come sweet." The mother responded, "I'm sorry, I must have forgotten the sugar." No amount of stirring will sweeten tea until the sugar is in it. And no amount of tireless human endeavor will bring unity to the church unless God's Spirit is in it. Mental orthodoxy is not the same as spiritual life. The creedal statement at Nicea was that the church was "one, holy, apostolic and catholic." The holy quality is dependent upon the Holy Spirit as are the marks of unity, apostolicity and catholicity.

In a convention speech, John W. Wade called attention to the slogan on the masthead of the magazine *Christian Standard*: "Devoted to the restoration of New Testament Christianity, its doctrine, its ordinances, and its fruit." Stressing the "fruit," he asked, "What does all this have to do with unity?" His answer was that it had everything to do with it. Then he prophesied:

For more than a century and a half we have, through theology

213

and reason, presented the plea for unity to the religious world about us. . . . None of us are completely satisfied with the past nor the prospects for the future. I am convinced that we will remain dissatisfied until we begin to give greater attention to the fruits of New Testament Christianity. We can talk Christian unity until the Lord returns, but unless we put some walk into our talk, the majority of the religious world will pay us but slight attention.

UNITY WILL COME TO THE "PENTECOSTAL" CONGREGATION

Again I use a word with a different meaning than is common parlance today. I do not refer to the modern practice termed "speaking in tongues." The present day experience of ecstatic speech does not appear to compare to the apostles' experience on Pentecost 30 A.D. Luke carefully describes the occurrence on that day, as the enablement of Galileans to declare "the wonders of God" in the "tongues," or the "languages" of the Jews that had come from countries across the Roman world (Acts 2:5-12).

When I speak of unity coming to a "Pentecostal" congregation, I mean that any congregation, that teaches or speaks "as the Spirit" gives utterance, will be enhancing oneness by limiting the teaching to God's revelation. On Pentecost the sermon exalted Jesus and told of his crucifixion and resurrection. The gospel always unifies. Preaching Jesus, like a magnet, draws his followers together. On Pentecost those inquiring, "What shall we do?" were given an answer that ought to be repeated at every evangelistic opportunity. The promise was not to be subject to varied answers from, "Ask Jesus into you heart," to "Your counsellor will help you give the sinner's prayer." It would be unifying, if every response followed that of the twelve apostles, "Repent and be baptized, every one of you . . . the promise is . . . for all whom the Lord our God will call" (Acts 2:37-39).

Alfred T. DeGroot, writing of unity in the thought of Alexander Campbell, saw that the key to unity was the key to conversion. He penned:

> The conditions upon which people are saved must necessarily be the conditions upon which the church should receive them; and if all churches will receive all persons who are thus qualified and no others, then all churches will have a common and interchangeable membership and sectarian barriers will no longer exist.

What a giant step toward unity could be taken if every gospel proclaimer would preach unchanged the conditions as stated by God's spokesman on the first day of the church.

The thoughts of God and those of men are not the same (Isa. 55:8). The mind of Christ, "God has revealed . . . by his Spirit. . . . This is what we speak, not in words taught us by human wisdom but in words taught by the Spirit" (I Cor. 2:10,13). To follow the teaching of "the sword of the Spirit, which is the word of God" (Eph. 6:17) is to be spiritual. To preach what the Spirit revealed and no other is the way to unity. To preach all that the Spirit revealed (Acts 20:27), without omission, will bring the congregations together.

A man, with a mountain stream running through his property, began raising ducks. He built stout pens to segregate different types of duck. The system of separation worked well until the flood waters caused the water level to rise higher than the pen fencing. The result was all the ducks were to be seen swimming together. May the outpouring to God's Spirit on his church lift us above the denominational coops that men have constructed to keep the Lord's people apart. Pray that a downpour from heaven come soon. "A cloud as small as a man's hand is rising from the sea" (I Kings 18:44). " 'There shall be showers of blessings:' Oh, that today they might fall," runs a line of prayer from El Nathan's hymn. We need the blessing of unity now. Sing that verse with a prayerful heart.

24

UNITY AND THE PLEASURE OF FELLOWSHIP

How large is your fellowship circle? Does it include too many and risk your witness to Biblical Christianity? Does it include too few and deplete the possibility of your full enjoyment of Christian oneness? If doctrinal purity is required for God to accept us, do we not need stand aloof from every brother in error? Making fellowship contingent upon correctness in all points, demands taking the road of exclusion, for when absolute correctness is the ultimate goal and exclusion is the route to the goal, division and separation are bound to occur. If no "heretic" is discernable immediately from whom to withdraw, a congregation is tempted to compensate by withdrawing from each other over some artificially created issue. Is enlarging fellowship a heavenly blessing or a mortal danger?

Fellowship means association, community or joint participation. The earliest church on record "devoted themselves . . . to the fellowship" (Acts 2:42) and were known to extend to others "the right hand of fellowship" (Gal. 2:9). The highest joy of a believer was to realize he had been "called (by God) . . . into fellowship with his Son Jesus Christ our Lord" (I Cor. 1:9). This "fellowship with the Spirit" (Phil. 2:1) was a "fellowship of sharing in his (Christ's) sufferings" (Phil. 3:10). Each redeemed person could exclaim, "Our fellowship is with the Father and with his Son, Jesus Christ" (I John 1:3). The "partnership in the gospel" (Phil. 1:5) was a bond between God and all his people, remembered at every "Participation in the blood of Christ" and "the body of Christ," as believers worshiped at the table of remembrance. (I Cor. 10:16-17).

THE UNDISCOVERED TREASURE

A condition of unity is association, for how can oneness survive in isolation, solitariness and separation? Isolation is debilitating. It impairs one's physical, mental and spiritual health. God the Father designed that we all have fellowship with him and all his other sons and daughters. Would it be carrying the principle of Matthew 25:40 too far to suggest that, when we cut ourselves off from the least of these, Christ's brethren — the other Christians, — we have cut ourselves off from Christ?

Where do we get the idea that fellowship with a mistaken brother is an endorsement of his mistakes? That notion long has been a barrier to unity. Fellowship is not the same as total approval. Our Lord did not become a sinner, when he associated with sinners. He did not become an endorsement of his twelve disciples' imperfect notions of the kingdom, just because he walked with them for three and a half years. You and I do not become denominationalists by associating with them. Perfection in understanding, life or teaching is not a condition of fellowship.

Agreement is neither an essential to, nor a prerequisite for, fellowship. It rather creates a proper atmosphere in which labor toward agreement has a better possibility for success. How can I

218

learn the outlook of separated brethern, if I never talk with them? "Accept one another, then, just as Christ accepted you" is the apostolic advice of Romans 15:7. "Disassociate yourself from one group of Christians, join yourself to a different group or start a new group," is the devil's counsel. Some in the Galatian churches were confused doctrinally by the Judaizers, but they were yet on Paul's list of brethren. Many in Corinth fell far short of what Christians ought to be, but they still received prime attention in the apostles' correspondence and prayers. Thessalonians were misinformed regarding true understanding of the Lord's return, but none of them were dropped from the rolls of those worthy of future contact. To build a sectarian wall around a Christian truth will not bear witness to that truth. It will rather take it out of circulation.

Beware of the temptation to monasticism and withdrawal from other believers. The motto, "We may not be large, but we are pure," is not approved in the Book from God. Christ envisioned his church as an interpersonal fellowship. He shared the fellowship, he had with the Father, with all who believed in him. Personal salvation through Christ was not individual redemption apart from the others so-rescued from sin. Christians are meant to enjoy interpersonal relationships with other believing individuals and congregations. Carl Gustav Jung could see that "the meeting of two personalities is like the contact of two chemical substances: if there is any reaction, both are transformed." A real transformation is certain to result, when Christians of different cultures, histories, and traditions, meet for the first time. The love of Christ and the depth of commitment to his kingdom found in persons, whose loyalty at first may have been questioned, may be a newly discovered treasure. You may find halos where you expected only horns. Prejudgment of another believer is never fair and is seldom true. When the facts are known, and the judgment is accurate that the brother is in error, the heavenly order still stands, "Accept him whose faith is weak, without passing judgment on disputable matters" (Rom. 14:1).

THE UNPARALLELED PLEASURE

Are we too busy building a wall around our own garden to make a path to where our religious neighbor has planted his roses? Joseph Newton believed, "People are lonely because they build walls instead of bridges." Our cold world needs warm-hearted Christians. There is truth in that song, "The more we get together the happier we'll be."

Forgive a personal testimony. Coming from the tradition with roots in the Campbell-Stone Movement, I attend regularly three Sunday services, one in each severed branch in that movement Christian Church, Church of Christ and Christian Church [Disciples of Christ]. I attempt to be present at national gatherings, such as the North American Christian Convention, the General Assembly of the Christian Church (Disciples of Christ) and the Pepperdine Lectures. Going to the regular minister's meeting of all the groups, I try to keep in touch, understand their positions and contribute to reunion efforts. My greatest pleasure is finding unquestioned commitment to the purpose of Christ in all. My annual efforts outside the Restoration Movement to teach Bible to congregational leaders in Eastern Europe (Brethren, Baptists, etc.) and the South Seas (Pentecostals, Congregationalists, etc.) have exposed me to the truth that many individuals wear human labels that do not declare really who they are. If the teaching given is clearly what the Bible says, "the sheep listen to his voice. . . . and his sheep follow him" (John 10:3-4).

How I would have robbed myself of some of life's richest joys, had I only been touched by the lives of a few saints rather than the many. Love demands encounters that are specific. To be united we must love one another and no one can love another he does not know and this knowing is preceded by meeting. You who are married remember how you first met. When you fell in love, nothing could keep you apart. Step one may never lead to step two, but step three can never happen until the first step is taken.

A Reader's Digest of long ago related the following item by G.S. Anderson:

> The new people next door were scarcely moved in when I found some of their mail pushed through my letter slot. I took it over to them and, in the process, made their acquaintance. A day or so later I saw another neighbor carrying mail to their house. The following morning I chided the postman for his carelessness. "Did you get to know the people?" he asked, his eyes twinkling. "Yes," I replied. "They're a nice couple." "Best way I know for people to get acquainted," he said.

Where can we find some more mail-carriers that will mix up the mail addressed to the many churches in your town? That might just get at least the ministers acquainted with each other. How can we encourage contact and mutual association?

Friendship with the friends of God is a hunger to be cultivated. Such a oneness will cease to exist, if it does not persist. Become suspicious of your fear to be contaminated by association with others who name Christ's name. Fear not. Join in the most challenging of all forms of mountain climbing, which is getting out of the rut of isolation.

THE UNFORGOTTEN MEASURE

If it concerns you to learn that I have always shared in the interdenominational minister's meetings in the cities where I preached, or that I still listen to lectures, delivered at the Society of Biblical Literature by liberals with whom I totally disagree, be assured that I do not ask you to follow my steps. I do, however, ask you to realize a basic element in the plea, "We are not the only Christians, but Christians only." That basic element is that there are Christians among the denominations. If that were not the case, our program would be to evangelize these pagans rather than unite the Christians within them by returning to New Testament faith and practice. I also ask you, in addition to sharing in the "untold pleasure" of an enlarged fellowship, to hold to the "unforgotten measure" — the standard of truth.

Alexander Campbell's now famous response to the sister from Lunenburg, began:

> If there be no Christians in the Protestant sects, there are certainly none among the Romanists, none among the Jews, Turks, Pagans, and therefore no Christians in the world except ourselves, or such of us as keep, or strive to keep, all the commandments of Jesus. Therefore, for many centuries there has been no church of Christ, no Christians in the world, and the promises concerning the *everlasting* kingdom of the Messiah have failed, and the *gates of hell have prevailed against his church!*"[1]

Isaac Errett, when Editor of the Christian Standard, pointed to the world of difference between the sects of Bible times and the denominations of his time. He wrote:

> That there is a very marked and fundamental distinction between the sects denounced in the Scriptures and these Protestant parties, must be conceded by every intelligent reader of history. Those broke away from the church of Christ — these from the church of Rome; those went *away from* the truth — these are coming back to it; those turned their backs to the authority of Christ, and set their faces to falsehood and delusion — these have turned their back to the pope, and set their faces to the Word of God and the cross of Christ. . . . How is it possible to place the latter in the same category with the former, unless *apostasy* and *reformation* mean the same thing?

Calling special attention to the apostolic norm, as the "reed like a measuring rod" (Rev. 11:1) by which we measure each teaching and practice in the church, William Robinson clarified:

> Our relationship to our brethren of denominational bodies must be a *de facto-de jure* relationship, i.e., *de facto*, we can all recognize each other's churchmanship whatever are the things

222

which divide us, but this does not mean that we say just anything is Christianity or Christian as if there were no objective thing, Christianity. What it does mean is that we are judges of no man's conscience and that we allow all to be as sincere as we ourselves claim to be, and further that we recognize the inevitability of the fact that through causes complex and baffling, many of which have their roots deep in history, the One Body of Christ appears today in broken fragments, a situation indeed sinful and the sinfulness of which we all bear in differing measures. But, *de jure* in those things which we claim to have discovered the true alignments of the one body and to have discarded accretions which are aberrations of original Christianity, we must stand firm within our borders until such time as we are proved to be wrong or as others discovering the right conform to the same practice. In this way, expediency does not triumph over principle. The recognition of this double attitude which is inevitable in the concrete situation avoids both wish-washiness and intolerance, both of which are enemies of true union.[2]

The wholesome desire to fellowship all born into the family of God, must not be misconstrued to mean any gospel, "which is really no gospel at all" (Gal. 1:7), is to be tolerated. Jesus commended the Ephesians who could "not tolerate . . . those who claim to be apostles but are not" (Rev. 2:2). He held no false toleration of the "Nicolaitans," "the synagogue of Satan," "the teaching of Balaam," nor the prophetess "Jezebel" (Rev. 2:6,9,14,20,24). To welcome Christ-denying, cross degrading teachers is to share in their "evil-work" (II John 10). There is a mistaken tolerance of differences, which is but a mask for indifference to the truth.

Christian fellowship, Biblically defined, is personal. You and I are true to the Scripture when we share with other Christians in every possible way that is consistent with our loyalty to Christ. No very young believer has the natural gift to pass an orthodoxy test with an A+ grade. All this proves that church fellowship cannot be restricted to common levels of Scriptural understanding. Approaches to all brethren will win more than reproaches of those same brethren.

Endnotes

1. *Millennial Harbinger*, 1837, p. 4ll.
2. *The Shattered Cross*, (Birmingham: Berean Press, 1948), p. 80.

CONCLUSION:

UNITY AND THE PRICE OF CHRIST-LIKENESS

Disciples of the Master Teacher must do more than audit the courses. One who audits a college course listens to the lectures but senses no burden to fulfill requirements or to do assignments. The Bible is the text-book on unity. We have read what it says. Together we believe what it teaches. What remains is to move from the status of auditor to enrollment as one who intends to do the required work, graduating from a mere professor of the faith to one who lives as Jesus instructs. "Faith without deeds is dead" (James 2:26). Moving from pleading for unity to practicing unity, will turn today's tragedy of a divided church into tomorrow's joy of a united one.

In the words of Halford E. Luccock, in the Beecher Lectures at Yale University, "No one can whistle a symphony. It takes an orchestra to play it." Will you join the orchestra of voices blending in oneness for the sake of Christian unity? Things are looking better. Robert McAfee Brown in an address in Pittsburg on March 4,

1965 demonstrated the slow but certain progress being made. He said,

> For a long time we hated one another. Then we ignored one another. Then we began talking about one another. Then we began talking to one another. Then we began praying for one another. And now we are beginning to pray with one another. And when that is a fact, no one can safely erect barriers around where the relationship may go from here.[1]

As the Bible teaches, "Let us consider how we may spur one another on toward love. . . . Let us not give up meeting together . . . let us encourage one another" (Heb. 10:24-25).

To learn that unity calls for love, humility, forgiveness, fellowship, patience, et al, is to see that in one word, "Christlikeness," is our need. Arguing about him must not be substituted for becoming like him. Jesus alone is "the way" (John 14:6) to unity. In him God's "grace and truth" combine (John 1:17). The more we become like him, the closer together we will become. Dean Stanley, long ago, taught:

> In the true, original, catholic, evangelical religion of Jesus Christ, and in this alone, all the divided religions of Christendom find their union, their repose, their support. Find out His mind, His character, His will; and in His greatness we shall rise above our littleness; in His strength we shall lose our weakness; in His peace we shall forget our discord.

Let us square up our lives by the model of his life. Every movement toward walking in his steps, will help us fulfill his class-assignment, "Be at peace with each other" (Mark 9:50).

To "fix our eyes on Jesus, the author and perfecter of our faith" (Heb. 12:2), is the only way to win the race against division. No less than Will Durant saw, "If Christianity would go back to its origins, cleanse itself resolutely from the silt of time, and take its stand with fresh sincerity upon the personality and ideals of its founder, who could resist it?"[2]

This book, *One Father, One Family* is a call to Christ-likeness. It is an appeal to move from casual Christianity to committed Christianity. It is a request for prayer for unity without ceasing and Bible study without creedal blinders. The book is a petition for personal repentance, where there has been but limited love for the brotherhood, and for personal patience, should the struggle for unity meet resistance.

It is time to roll-up our sleeves and do the hard-work required. It is the hour for kneeling in prayer for the grace that will enable us to make "the most of every opportunity" (Eph. 5:16) in reaching a world that is ready to accept Jesus; but is not open to the creedal and hierarchical systems that sometimes hide him. It is the day to follow the path infallibly right and exceedingly simple — the way of being totally Christian, but just a Christian.

If you wonder whether being a Christian only is possible, the answer is "Yes, indeed!" The first years of the church knew of no "Protestant-Christian" or "Catholic-Christians." Millions today are simply Christians. You can be too.

> The world and the devil can chide us
> Because of the names that divide us;
> And well may they mock and deride us
>   When party names number two hundred.
> One Bible is all the Lord gave us;
> One Faith all-sufficient to save us;
> One Lord who redeemed and forgave us;
>   But what of the two hundred names?
>
> While the cynical world now can revel
> And mock and deride with the devil,
> It isn't all quite on the level —
>   The Lord never made the two hundred.
> He founded one church to redeem us;
> Not two hundred such to blaspheme us;
> But thus does the world now esteem us —
>   With party names over two hundred.

There's naught in the name, they all tell us,
But party names do make us jealous;
And thousands who think they are zealous
    Are but jealous for some party name.
Why not wear just the name of the Master?
The lost world would find Him the faster,
And save us the pain and disaster
    Of jealousy over the name.

And creeds — human creeds — how confusing!
More pathetic, indeed, than amusing.
Two hundred to sift for the choosing
    Of one that is suited to me.
I can not begin to compare them,
Much less to do aught to repair them
But this I can do: I can spare them
    For the one that the Book has for me.

I endorse it without alteration,
Accept it without reservation —
The simple, divine revelation
    That Jesus the Christ is God's Son.
His name is the creed that is given
To bring us to God and to heaven;
For in Him all our sins are forgiven —
    Because we confess Him, God's Son.

Men's mouthing of creeds may divide us,
And dogmas confuse and misguide us;
But the Book of all books would still guide us
    To the oneness in Christ Jesus' name.
We can speak where the Bible has spoken;
Where silent, leave silence unbroken
ONE CHURCH would then stand as a token
    Of Jesus' divine, saving name.[3]

Endnotes

1. Quoted in Ralph Louis Woods, Editor, *The World Treasury of Religious Quotations*, (New York: Hawthorn Books, 1966), p. 1022.

2. "The Crisis in Christianity" in the *Saturday Evening Post*, August 5, 1939.

3. C. A. Boulton, *"A Divided Church."* This poem appeared in *The Lookout* many years ago.

Index of Names

231

Index of Topics

Index of Scriptures

239

ONE FATHER, ONE FAMILY